SEEING JAZZ

AS FROM MY WINDOW I SOMETIMES GLANCE...

Eugene Smith
silver gelatin print
1957-58

SEEING JAZZ

ARTISTS AND WRITERS ON JAZZ

Foreword by Clark Terry

Introduction by Robert O'Meally

Afterword by Milt Hinton

Compiled by

Marquette Folley-Cooper   Deborah Macanic   Janice McNeil

Edited by Elizabeth Goldson

Chronicle Books in association with the Smithsonian Institution Traveling Exhibition Service

Published by Chronicle Books on the occasion of an exhibition organized
by the Smithsonian Institution Traveling Exhibition Service as part of
America's Jazz Heritage, A Partnership of the Lila Wallace-Reader's Digest
Fund and the Smithsonian Institution.

AMERICA'S

HERITAGE

Book design: Elixir
Manufactured in China

Library of Congress Cataloging-in-Publication Data:
Seeing Jazz: artists and writers on jazz / foreword by Clark Terry;
    introduction by Robert O'Meally; afterword by Milt Hilton;
    compiled by Marquette Folley-Cooper, Deborah Macanic,
    Janice McNeil; edited by Elizabeth Goldson.
        p. cm.
    Includes index.
    ISBN 0-8118-1732-6 (Pb) ISBN 0-8118-1180-8 (HC)
    1. Jazz in art. 2. Jazz in literature.
I. Folley-Cooper, Marquette. II. Macanic, Deborah.
III. McNeil, Janice. IV. Goldson, Elizabeth.
V. Smithsonian Institution.
    Traveling Exhibition Service.
    ML85.S38   1997
    700'.457–dc21   97-5084
                                          CIP
                                          MN

Distributed in Canada by Raincoast Books
9050 Shaughnessy Street
Vancouver, B.C. V6P 6E5

10 9 8 7 6 5 4 3

Chronicle Books LLC, 85 Second Street, San Francisco, CA 94105
www.chroniclebooks.com

CONTENTS

FOREWORD

Art has to do with the inner emotions of the person who is presenting it. An artist must be capable of giving vent to his or her feelings; nothing reaches the point of being artistic until it touches the soul.

There are so many artists who interpret the jazz language. Musicians, of course, and painters, sculptors, and poets too. The colors, the structures, the stories they tell share a certain power of expression. One splash of a Chagall can sound like Bird. And Picasso, he was a swinger. You can recognize any figure he drew because it automatically swings, just like Dizzy.

An artistic person can express himself in a number of ways. Pops [Louis Armstrong] used to say that anyone who could play a horn could sing, because the language of jazz could be spoken the same way with the voice as with an instrument. Duke Ellington said that he would never hire a musician who couldn't dance, because he wanted players who understood rhythm and could "make a phrase dance." I know many musicians who paint, many people who can look at an object and see the music in it, or listen to music and hear its colors. When I read poetry by someone like Langston Hughes, I hear the beat and imagine the words as a song. All forms of creativity in jazz—all of the music, all of the words and images in this book—are about having something to express, something artistic to say, however one chooses to say it.

My own inspiration comes from beautiful people that I meet and work with and from beautiful music that I have the opportunity to play. I think about how marvelous it has been for me to have known the people who created the music: people like Duke Ellington, Ella Fitzgerald, Count Basie, and Dizzy Gillespie, just to name a few. To be able to perpetuate the craft that these people started is a blessing and an inspiration.

Musicians are also inspired by their audiences. You can sense when you have an audience that is mature and hip about jazz. It's wonderful to invite people into this enjoyable world, to open their eyes and their minds, to show them where they can find some satisfaction, some happiness, some beauty they didn't have before. Welcome inside the sphere of jazz.

Clark Terry

INTRODUCTION

The title *Seeing Jazz* is a layered play on words that refers to the artistic and literary works here as visualizations of music—visible equivalents to the sound of jazz—and also to "seeing" in the metaphoric sense of understanding: to get hip and then hipper, to hear jazz more deeply than ever before, to dig this music, to say "yes, I *see.*"

Seeing Jazz presents jazz music as an expression of the United States in the 20th century—the music of *e pluribus unum* with a swinging beat—and as a multicolored blue cornerstone of what the world knows as *modernism* in art. As such, this music has had an impact on many other modern musics, at home and abroad, "classical" as well as "popular." Jazz is part of a super-charged cultural continuum in which painters, sculptors, photographers, poets, novelists, and essayists have worked (and played) to capture with their pens and brushes, their wood and paper, and with light the irresistible note and trick and dance of the music. This book reflects in jam-session style the creation of the still-emerging jazz culture, in which the music is a constant point of reference and sounding board:

jazz, the lowdown high-fly music of inspiration and perfection in form.

How does one begin to define this music that was born in the port towns and big cities of black America and adopted by the world as its own? From the earliest shy flights of James Reese Europe's military "jass" bands of the 1910s to the latest experiments by bold jazz innovators, three aspects of jazz have emerged as definitive: complexity of *rhythm,* the magic of *improvisation,* and conversational *call and response.* These terms provide the title and theme for each of the three chapters in this book.

Seeing Jazz is an evocative experiment— a place to begin, not the last word. It is not an encyclopedic effort to gather all of the jazz paintings and poems from around the world and across the century of this music's existence. Rather it is a playful attempt to illustrate how this music has made its cross-disciplinary mark. It also endeavors to capture the full-spirited extravagance of joy so unmistakable in the music; it strives to *swing.*

Robert O'Meally

DRUM THING (NO BLUES FOR ELVIN)

James Phillips
acrylic on paper
1995

RHYTHM

Examples of *rhythm* veer toward the mystical: the first thunders that drummed the world into being, the dance of the spheres and of the sea, the ebb and flow of desire and procreation, the cadence of blood through human veins. Jazz music's rhythms echo these primal sounds along with those of its origins as an American music owing debts to Europe, Asia, Native America, and Africa—especially Africa, where the music's polyrhythmic character and drum and dance-beat attitudes found their beginnings.

Jazz crystallized at the turn of the 19th to the 20th century in the black communities of the United States, and if we listen closely as Sidney Bechet advises, we hear its history deeply drumming. We hear spirituals, blues, vendor's cries, marching bands, street corner idlers telling lies. We hear the sound of trains—wheels on tracks, whistles, brakes, conductors' calls, easy (and uneasy) riders. In the music of Mary Lou Williams, for example, we hear modern city rhythms—steady and swinging in one instance, barbwire jagged and discontinuous in the next.

The rhythms of jazz have also inspired poets and visual artists. Both depict the drama of jazz players in action. Both accept the harder task of capturing in line and image the feeling and the meaning of the music. Both *see* jazz and make their audiences see it, too.

But how does one *see* jazz in this sense? How does one *write* or *draw* the rhythms of this music? Writers like Toni Morrison, Ntozake Shange, Amiri Baraka, Albert Murray, Michael Harper, and Rita Dove (just to name some leaders in the literary jazz aesthetic) not only tell the stories of jazz characters but pace their lines to approximate the dance-beat cadences and other rhythmic features of jazz music. Through playfully syncopated repetitions, their words perform a jazz dance on the page. No wonder Langston Hughes specified that one of his books, *Ask Your Mama,* be read aloud to jazz accompaniment; the words for him were solo notes sounded and scored in a jazz-rhythm pattern.

Through much of the century, visual artists literally have drawn jazz musicians, dancers, instruments, and sheet music. Henri Matisse, Piet Mondrian, and Jean Dubuffet make jazz music sound through their paintings, make us *see* the music. These and many others have created visual jazz compositions through their manipulation of *lines, figures, tones, structures, colors,* and *rhythms.* Note how the language of aesthetics overlaps from art form to art form. In some sense, do not all artists—whether dancers or architects, sculptors or poets—desire that their works have rhythm?

In visual art, a jazz rhythm may be visible in repeated images or human figures (with variations from image to image). Thus do the artists follow jazz's impulse to play 4/4 along with 3/4 or 6/8, to mirror jazz's complexly swinging, polyrhythmic character. Like writers, some visual artists divide their work into sections that approximate the structures of jazz: the A section swinging into the B section and back to A before on to C (the *vamp, chorus, riff, solo space, outchorus,* etc.) with rhythm always at the base. Stuart Davis and Romare Bearden describe the effort to achieve a sense of the *jazz interval* in their works, the *skip tones, jump spaces,* and silences in anticipation of the next sound. Others achieve a percussive sense of color—jazz drum songs for the eye.

Perhaps most profoundly, writers and visual artists who project jazz rhythms into their art express a jazz timekeeper's base-clef sense of life. The feeling, as Ralph Ellison once put it, that as blues-beset as life may be (look at the photo of Billie Holiday) the real secret is somehow to make life *swing,* to survive by staying in the groove. *Look at the photo of Billie Holiday.*

Robert O'Meally

CAROLINA SHOUT

William T. Williams
acrylic on canvas
1990

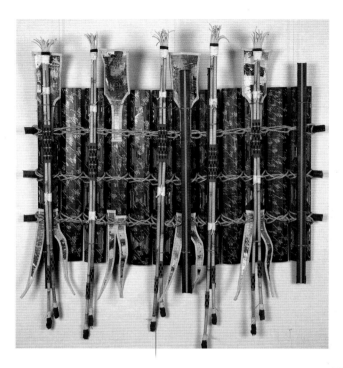

This music accepts repetition as an already accepted fact of life. You breathe, your heart beats, quickens with the music's pulse, and yours...your foot pats, these are the things we don't even think about. The point then is to *move* it away from what we already know, toward, into, what we only *sense*. Music is for the senses. Music should make you *feel*. But, finally, unless you strip yourself of outside interference, almost all your reactions will be *social*.

But the point of living seems to me to get to your actual feelings, as, say, these musicians want always to get to theirs. If you can find out who you are (you're no thing), then you can find out what you feel. Because we *are* our feelings, or our lack of them.

The music, possible feeling, is here. Where ever you are. All you have to do is listen. Listen!

BEMBÉ CLAVÉ

Al Smith
mixed media
1994

from BLACK MUSIC

LeRoi Jones / Amiri Baraka

BLACK SWAN SUITE

Peter Wayne Lewis
oil on canvas
1993

COZY COLE, DANNY BARKER, AND SHAD COLLINS, NEW ORLEANS

Milt Hinton

photograph

c.1941

It's not just rhythm; it's a language.

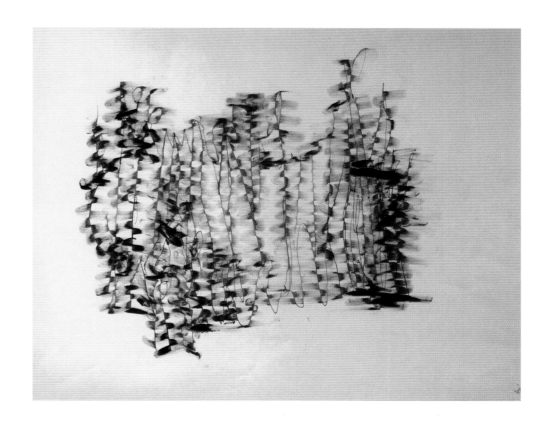

from MI GENTE

Andy González
quoted by Blanca Vázquez

UNTITLED (SKETCH TO CHARLIE PARKER'S MUSIC)

Norman Lewis
pen, ink, and wash on paper
1949

Ragtime, it's the musicianers. *Rag it up*, we used to say. You take any piece, you make it so people can dance to it, pat their feet, move around. You make it so they can't help themselves from doing that. You make it so they just can't sit still. And that's all there is to it. It's the rhythm there. The rhythm *is* ragtime. That's still there to be done. You could do that to all kinds of numbers still being played, still being composed today.

That rhythm goes all the way back. In the spirituals the people clapped their hands—that was their rhythm. In the blues it was further down; they didn't need the clapping, but they remembered it, it was still there. And both of them, the spirituals and the blues, they was a prayer. One was praying to God and the other was praying to what's human. It's like one was saying, "Oh, God, let me go," and the other was saying, "Oh, Mister, let me be." And they were both the same thing in a way; they were both my people's way of praying to be themselves, praying to be let alone so they could be human. The spirituals, they had a kind of trance to them, a kind of forgetting. It was like a man closing his eyes so he can see a light inside him. That light, it's far off and you've got to wait to see it. But it's there. It's waiting. The spirituals, they're a way of seeing that light. It's a far off music; it's a going away, but it's a going away that takes you with it. And the blues, they've got that sob inside, that awful lonesome feeling. It's got so much remembering inside it, so many bad things to remember, so many losses.

But both of them, they're based on rhythm. They're both of them leading up to a rhythm. And they're both coming up from a rhythm. It's like they're going and coming at the same time. Going, coming—inside the music that's the same thing, it's the rhythm. And that rhythm and that feeling you put around it, always keeping the melody, that's all there is to it. That's nothing that's dead. That's nothing that could die: 1910, 1923, 1950—there's no difference in that. And to give you what this Jazz is—all you need is a few men who can hear what the man next him is doing at the same time that you know your instrument and how you can say on it what you gotta say to keep the next man going with you, leading one another on to the place the music has to go.

GRAND JAZZ BAND (NEW ORLEANS)

Jean Dubuffet
oil and tempera on canvas
1944

from TREAT IT GENTLE

Sidney Bechet

SWEET EMMA BARRETT

Lee Friedlander
silver gelatin print
1958

YELLOW DOG BLUES

Douglas Vogel
mixed media with electric light
1995

Because the also and also of all of that was also the also plus also of so many of the twelve-bar twelve-string guitar riddles you got whether in idiomatic iambics or otherwise mostly from Luzana Cholly who was the one who used to walk his trochaic-sporty stomping-ground limp-walk picking and plucking and knuckle knocking and strumming (like an anapestic locomotive) while singsongsaying Anywhere I hang my hat anywhere I prop my feet. Who could drink muddy water who could sleep in a hollow log.

from **TRAIN WHISTLE GUITAR**

Albert Murray

BLACK AND TAN

Mark Faber
mixed media
1994

WITH STRINGS PART 2

Jean-Michel Basquiat
acrylic and mixed media on canvas
1983

It all began with the cord

between the fingers.

Its sound

penetrated even the bottom of the soul,

and there it remained.

Later came the drum,

marvelous, rhythmic, sensual.

Its sound vibrated between my hands, and

entered the center of the heart;

And there it stayed.

Inside me,

coexist the cord and the drum.

They have their abode in my soul,

and they permit me, on

hot nights,

to talk with the moon

and the stars.

THE CORD BETWEEN THE FINGERS

Helio Orovio

WILL SHADE AND HIS TUB BASS, MEMPHIS

William Claxton
silver gelatin print
1960

NEW ORLEANS FAREWELL

Romare Bearden
collage
1974

It was really a question of that: the best strutter in the club, he'd be the Grand Marshal. He'd be a man who could prance when he walked, a man that could really fool and surprise you. He'd keep time to the music, but all along he'd keep a strutting and moving so you'd never know what he was going to be doing next. Naturally, the music, it makes you strut, but it's *him* too, the way he's strutting, it gets you. It's what you want from a parade: you want to *see* it as well as hear it. And all those fancy steps he'd have— oh, that was really something!—ways he'd have of turning around himself. People, they got a whole lot of pleasure out of just watching him, hearing the music and seeing him strut and other members of the club coming behind him, strutting and marching, some riding on horses but getting down to march a while, gallivanting there in real style. It would have your eyes just the same as your ears for waiting.

from **TREAT IT GENTLE**
Sidney Bechet

It was a very famous entrance you know. He walks out of the crowd, struggles through onto the street and begins playing, too loud but real and strong you couldn't deny him, and then he went back into the crowd. Then fifteen minutes later, 300 yards down the street, he jumps through the crowd onto the street again, plays, and then goes off. After two or three times we were waiting for him and he came.

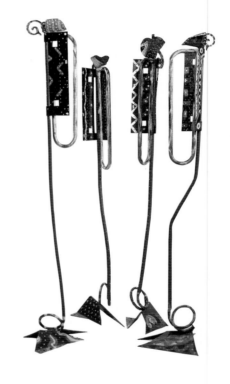

from COMING THROUGH SLAUGHTER

Michael Ondaatje

THE STRUTTERS

Ed Love
polychromed welded steel
1986

BAND MEMBER AT BEBÉ RIDGLEY'S FUNERAL

Hermenegildo Sábat

photograph

1961

EDDIE PALMIERI

Ricardo Betancourt
photographs
1993

Now I have one radio-phonograph; I plan to have five. There is a certain acoustical deadness in my hole, and when I have music I want to *feel* its vibration, not only with my ear but with my whole body. I'd like to hear five recordings of Louis Armstrong playing and singing "What Did I Do to Be so Black and Blue"—all at the same time. Sometimes now I listen to Louis while I have my favorite dessert of vanilla ice cream and sloe gin. I pour the red liquid over the white mound, watching it glisten and the vapor rising as Louis bends that military instrument into a beam of lyrical sound. Perhaps I like Louis Armstrong because he's made poetry out of being invisible. I think it must be because he's unaware that he *is* invisible. And my own grasp of invisibility aids me to understand his music. Once when I asked for a cigarette, some jokers gave me a reefer, which I lighted when I got home and sat listening to my phonograph. It was a strange evening. Invisibility, let me explain, gives one a slightly different sense of time, you're never quite on the beat. Sometimes you're ahead and sometimes behind. Instead of the swift and imperceptible flowing of time, you are aware of its nodes, those points where time stands still or from which it leaps ahead. And you slip into the breaks and look around. That's what you hear vaguely in Louis' music.

Once I saw a prizefighter boxing a yokel. The fighter was swift and amazingly scientific. His body was one violent flow of rapid rhythmic action. He hit the yokel a hundred times while the yokel held up his arms in stunned surprise. But suddenly the yokel, rolling about in the gale of boxing gloves, struck one blow and knocked science, speed and footwork as cold as a well-digger's posterior. The smart money hit the canvas. The long shot got the nod. The yokel had simply stepped inside of his opponent's sense of time. So under the spell of the reefer I discovered a new analytical way of listening to music. The unheard sounds came through, and each melodic line existed of itself, stood out clearly from all the rest, said its piece, and waited patiently for the other voices to speak.

from **INVISIBLE MAN**

Ralph Ellison

I am
in the mean
hot
cold
warm
red
purple
blue
high
deep
low
middle

IN THE MIDDLE

Abbey Lincoln

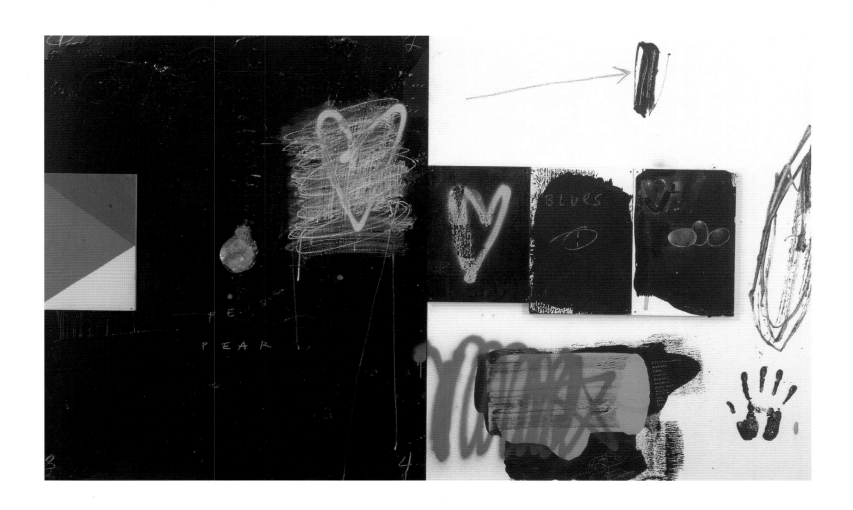

BLUES, RED, YELLOW II (HOMAGE TO BILLIE HOLIDAY)

Raymond Saunders
oil, mixed media on wood
1990

BILLIE HOLIDAY

Dennis Stock
photograph
1958

for Michael S. Harper

Billie Holiday's burned voice
had as many shadows as lights,
a mournful candelabra against a sleek piano,
the gardenia her signature under that ruined face.

(Now you're cooking, drummer to bass,
magic spoon, magic needle.
Take all day if you have to
with your mirror and your bracelet of song.)

Fact is, the invention of women under siege
has been to sharpen love in the service of myth.

If you can't be free, be a mystery.

CANARY

Rita Dove

When we weren't on the road, we spent most of our time around Kansas City, and there were after-hours sessions every night. They were something else. A good one went right through the next day. Style didn't matter. What mattered was to keep the thing going. I'd stop in at a session after work, and they would be doing "Sweet Georgia Brown." I'd go home and take a bath and change my dress, and when I got back—an hour or more later—they'd still be on "Georgia Brown." Ben Webster came and threw some gravel on the window screen one night and woke me and my husband up and asked my husband if I could come to a session, because they were out of piano players. I went down, and Coleman Hawkins was there—Fletcher Henderson was in town—and he was having a bad time. He was down to his undershirt, and sweating and battling for his life against Lester Young and Herschel Evans and Ben, too. But they weren't cutting sessions. I recall Chu Berry sitting out front at a session and listening and not moving. When he got on the stand, he repeated note for note the last chorus the man before him had played—just to show how much he admired it—and then he went into his own bag.

from OUT HERE AGAIN

Mary Lou Williams
quoted by Whitney Balliett

MARY LOU WILLIAMS AT HER PIANO

Dennis Stock
photograph
1958

Pres

   spoke in a language

"of his own." What did he say, between the

horn line

s, pork pie hat

tenor tilted

pres once was a drummer but gave it up cause other dudes

  was getting

the foxes

while he packed his tomtoms

"Ding Dong," pres sd, meaning

like a typewriter, its the end

of this

line. "No Eyes," pres wd say, meaning

I didn't cdn't dig it, and what it was was

lame. Pres

had a language

and a life, like,

all his own,

but in the teeming whole of us he lived

toooting on his sideways horn

translating frankie trumbauer into

Bird's feathers

Tranes sinewy tracks

the slickster walking through the crowd

surviving on a terrifying wit

its the jungle the jungle the jungle

we living in

and cats like pres cd make it because they were clear they, at

  least,

had to,

to do anything else.

Save all that comrades, we need it.

PRES SPOKE IN A LANGUAGE

LeRoi Jones / Amiri Baraka

The rhythm of life
Is a jazz rhythm,
Honey.
The gods are laughing at us.

from LENOX AVENUE: MIDNIGHT

Langston Hughes

ART TATUM

Morgan Monceaux
mixed media
1991

FREEDOM'S GATE

Charles Searles
bronze
1992

STRIVING

Charles Searles
bronze
1994

WARRIOR

Charles Searles
bronze
1992

The last time I talked with him, the reddish-brown-skinned baritone recalled being a Southern kid on his bicycle more than fifty years ago and seeing posters that announced the arrival of the greatest band in the world. He told of a magical afternoon in Mississippi and of pedalling out to the train station, where he heard the sound of Duke Ellington's brass men warming up, the light hitting those silver or golden horns through which they eased so much heat and sophisticated feeling. Then he spoke of looking through the windows at the Ellingtonians, inside the private Pullman cars that sat on those Mississippi train tracks like luxury hotel rooms on wheels. He remembered the spit and polish of the Negro men who were serving them, in movements swift but casual with authority. There were also thrilled and thrilling women there, all those fine brown felines visiting the artists who set the romantic standards for men from coast to coast, border to border.

That night, in the company of what was obviously an unforgettable brown-skinned beauty, Earl attended the dance where Ellington's band was performing. Negroes took to the floor on every tune, and whites sat behind ropes, enjoying Ellington's music and the floor show of romance and rhythm so superbly provided by the local people who became, in Dizzy Gillespie's words, "the mirrors of the music." Earl remembered that during intermission the smooth-looking Ellington sat at a table with the whites who ran the town, but that he sat not as the target of a joke or as some version of inferiority. He charmed and laughed and told tales as a man of talent and aristocratic bearing whose humanity took a back seat to no one's.

I now understand that whenever I heard Coleman sing or sat down with the man or spoke with him on the phone, he was always savoring that moment as a Mississippi dreamer in his teens, back down the staircase of time to the point where he saw just how far real talent could take someone, no matter where on the social spectrum that someone had come from. As a romantic balladeer, even on those cold, cold blue nights when he was standing in the gutter, Earl Coleman was surely looking at the stars.

from EARL AND THE DUKE

Stanley Crouch

THE EYE OF THE HORN (Wynton Marsalis)

Lynn Goldsmith
Mamiya
1993

Art affirms plastically
the ancient truth that
life is equilibrated
rhythm. Art always
realizes this equilibrium
in life.

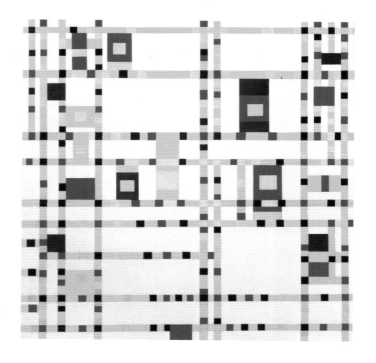

from **THE NEW ART—THE NEW LIFE**

Piet Mondrian

BROADWAY BOOGIE WOOGIE

Piet Mondrian
oil on canvas
1942-43

Imploring Mecca
to achieve
six discs
with Decca.

One thousand saxophones infiltrate the city,
Each with a man inside,
Hidden in ordinary cases,
Labeled FRAGILE.

A fleet of trumpets drops their hooks,
Inside at the outside.

Ten waves of trombones approach the city
Under blue cover
Of late autumn's neo-classical clouds.

Five hundred bassmen, all string feet tall,
Beating it back to the bass.

One hundred drummers, each a stick in each hand,
The delicate rumble of pianos, moving in.

The secret agent, an innocent bystander,
Drops a note in the wail box.

Five generals, gathered in the gallery,
Blowing plans.

At last, the secret code is flashed:
Now is the time, now is the time.

Attack: The sound of jazz.

The city falls.

BE-BOP BOYS

Langston Hughes

BATTLE REPORT

Bob Kaufman

OOP-POP-A-DA

Billy Dee Williams
mixed media on paper
1994

SING PRAISES

Denise Ward-Brown
assemblage
1993

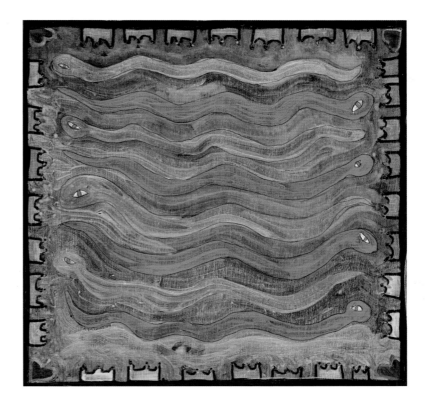

It is enough to open your eyes to the April rainbow

And the ears, above all the ears to God who with a burst of

    saxophone laughter created the heavens and the earth

    in six days

And on the seventh day, he slept his great negro sleep.

from **NEW YORK (JAZZ ORCHESTRA: SOLO TRUMPET)**

Léopold Sédar Senghor

THE ORIGINAL MAMBO KINGS

Michelle Cartaya
mixed media
1993

God breathes through us so completely... so gently we

hardly feel it... yet, it is our everything.

Thank you God

ELATION—ELEGANCE—EXALTATION—

All from God.

Thank you God. Amen.

Soul and race
are private dominions,
memories and modal
songs, a tenor blossoming,
which would paint suffering
a clear color but is not in
this Victorian house
without oil in zero degree
weather and a forty-mile-an-hour wind;
it is all a well-knit family:
a love supreme.
Oak leaves pile up on walkway
and steps, catholic as apples
in a special mist of clear white
children who love my children.
I play "Alabama"
on a warped record player
skipping the scratches
on your faces over the fibrous
conical hairs of plastic
under the wooden floors.

Dreaming on a train from New York
to Philly, you hand out six
notes which become an anthem
to our memories of you:
oak, birch, maple,
apple, cocoa, rubber.
For this reason Martin is dead;
For this reason Malcolm is dead;
for this reason Coltrane is dead;
in the eyes of my first son are the browns
of these men and their music.

from **A LOVE SUPREME**

John Coltrane
from the liner notes

HERE WHERE COLTRANE IS

Michael Harper

ALABAMA

Ed Love
welded steel
1993

IMPROVISATION

The word *improvisation* derives from the Latin *im + provisus,* meaning "not provided" or "not foreseen." In some sense, all artistic creation depends on the ability to improvise, to extemporize an unscripted drama, to blow a note not heard before, to fill the blank canvas of the moment. But in the making of jazz music, improvisation is a definitive hallmark, a *sine qua non:* a something without which, *not.* Jazz is substantially a performer's art where any charts or notations are provisional guideposts, notes indicating a work's general direction but never its final lines or last word. It is a music in the oral tradition, one in which a composer/arranger's latest changes may be shouted out during on-stage performance and where the performer may introduce a shift in direction while playing, in the unforeseen moment of jazz creation.

Jazz's improvised character is balanced with the fact that it is never a free-for-all; it has both an improvised freshness as well as a composer/arranger's sense of completeness and finish. Duke Ellington told his band to play the notes as written but also "to keep some dirt in there, somewhere." In other words, even when Ellington's band played pieces with no solo spaces indicated, he wanted his players to keep the made-up-on-the-spot dimension, something the score expected but did not ask for explicitly, something of the performers' improvised own, some "dirt."

At their best, jazz compositions sound like frozen improvisations, just as solos by such jazz artists as Thelonious Monk and Miles Davis sound like liquid compositions. The jazz improvisor's solo statement not only tells the soloist's own story (see Gwendolyn Brooks' poem on this subject) but must complement the composer/arranger's overall conceptions. In other words, true jazz musicians are co-composers of every work they play.

The audience delights just as much in a particular composition as in a particular band's or player's treatment of it on a given day.

All of which has implications and challenges for the other arts. The sculptors, painters, photographers, and authors whose works appear here also operate *in the moment.* Romare Bearden insisted that, like a jazz soloist, he played with the possibilities within the framework of his conception: he soloed, he improvised. Jean-Michel Basquiat, Alexis De Boeck, and others gave their work a swingingly improvised dimension. They kept "some dirt in there, somewhere," too.

This in-the-moment quality is most obvious in the work of jazz photographers like William Claxton, Herman Leonard, and Anthony Barboza. Like jazz players, jazz photographers must be so well trained that they can see an image, have an idea, and execute instantly. As Ornette Coleman advises, they "forget about the changes in key and just play." And when it comes to jazz art (musical, literary, or visual) the ability to play is the thing. Technique, however painfully hard earned, is taken for granted and "forgotten." When the bandleader points to you, can you create a composition on the spot? With little or nothing formally provided, are you composed? Can you improvise? Can you play?

Robert O'Meally

JAZZ

Man Ray
tempera and ink (aerograph) on paper
c. 1919

Forget about the changes in key and just play within the range of the idea.

from FOUR LIVES IN THE BEBOP BUSINESS

Ornette Coleman
quoted by A.B. Spellman

GREAT EXPECTATIONS

Laura Thorne
mixed media
1995

MORNING NOTE

Letizia Pitigliani
acrylic on canvas
1989

BLACK MANHATTAN

Romare Bearden
collage and synthetic polymer on board
1969

Think how it is, if you can manage, just manage it. Nature freaks for you, then. Turns itself into shelter, byways. Pillows for two. Spreads the limbs of lilac bushes low enough to hide you. And the City, in its own way, gets down for you, cooperates, smoothing its sidewalks, correcting its curbstones, offering you melons and green apples on the corner. Racks of yellow head scarves; strings of Egyptian beads. Kansas fried chicken and something with raisins call attention to an open window where the aroma seems to lurk. And if that's not enough, doors to speakeasies stand ajar and in that cool dark place a clarinet coughs and clears its throat waiting for the woman to decide on the key. She makes up her mind and as you pass by informs your back that she is daddy's little angel child. The City is smart at this: smelling and good and looking raunchy; sending secret messages disguised as public signs: this way, open here, danger to let colored only single men on sale woman wanted private room stop dog on premises absolutely no money down fresh chicken free delivery fast. And good at opening locks, dimming stairways. Covering your moans with its own.

from JAZZ

Toni Morrison

Do you remember driving into the City? From Philly over the bridges into Jersey. Flat out up the pike then the tunnel. Didn't it seem everybody going our way, headed for the same place? All those cars and trucks and buses, man. Planes in the air. Trains. Close to Newark you could even see ocean liners. Every damn form of transportation known to man, man. And every kind of high. All making it to the City. Unanimous. The people's choice. And you were there in that number. Doing it, boy. Shoom. Kicking the Jersey turnpike. Pedal to the metal. Radio already there and sending back waves. Chasing. Chased. Won't it be something when all these folks pour down through the tunnel and we're each and all of us packed into the same tight squeeze of our destination. The Five Spot. Lintons. The Village Gate. Miracle of planes trains buses cars ships arriving and checking in and checking out the scene. I can't wait. Nobody can.

from **CONCERT**

John Edgar Wideman

PAD NO. 4

Stuart Davis

silk-screen reproduction

1947

ADDISON AND ART FARMER

Robert Parent
silver gelatin print
1955

Each thing you hear

determines the direction

that you go. You just follow the music,

and if you follow the music you

can go anywhere.

from **THE MAN WITH THE STRAIGHT HORN**

Steve Lacy
quoted by Richard Scott

CHET BAKER AND TEDDY CHARLES, PASADENA

William Claxton
silver gelatin print
1953

IN E SHARP

Romare Bearden
oil and collage on paper
1981

Some years ago, I showed a watercolor to Stuart Davis, and he pointed out that I had treated both the left and right sides of the painting in exactly the same way. After that, at Davis's suggestion, I listened for hours to recordings of Earl Hines at the piano. Finally, I was able to block out the melody and concentrate on the silences between the notes. I found that this was very helpful to me in the transmutation of sound into colors and the placement of objects in my paintings and collages.

from REMINISCENCES

Romare Bearden

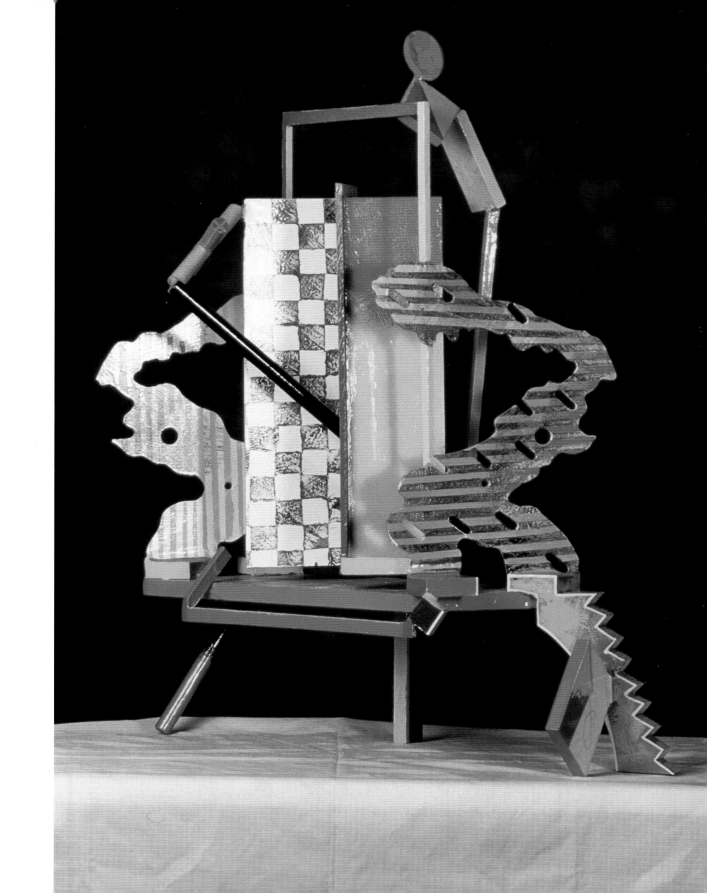

STAGE DOOR NO EXIT

John T. Scott
polychromed aluminum
1995

i live in music

is this where you live

i live here in music

i live on c♯ street

my friend lives on b♭ avenue

do you live here in music

sound

falls round me like rain on other folks

saxophones wet my face

cold as winter in st. louis

hot like peppers i rub on my lips

thinkin they waz lilies

i got 15 trumpets where other women got hips

& a upright bass for both sides of my heart

i walk round in a piano like somebody

else/be walkin on the earth

i live in music

    live in it

       wash in it

i cd even smell it

wear sound on my fingers

sound falls   so fulla music

ya cd make a river where yr arm is &

hold yrself

      hold yrself in a music

I LIVE IN MUSIC

Ntozake Shange

ANITA O'DAY

Dennis Stock

photograph

1958

ICARUS (PLATE VIII FROM JAZZ)

Henri Matisse
pochoir, printed in color
1947

1.

ive been dancing all my life
probably came out of the womb doing a little step
ive danced on 4 continents plus several islands
in places hifly la la la & lowdown lowlife ummmph
i got a dance major masters degree
someones even doing a thesis on me
danced solo duet trio quartet & ensemble with my own dance company
with music
without music
even got rave reviews in the new york times
but more than anything else ive always wanted to dance with sun ra
now hes left this planet
guess i gotta wait til we meet somewhere over there on the other side of
space is the place space is the place space

4b.

me & sun ra
when we do our duet
just me & sun ra
i am gonna do it like this
thats good for the duet dont you think
then when i do it with the arkestra
with sun ra & the whole big myth science arkestra live!
& me
i am gonna do it like this
"from planet to planet"
& like this
& like this
& then "from planet to planet"
i am gonna
gonna
gonna
"from planet to planet"
gonna
"from planet to planet"

5.

s u n   r a
sunny
a/k/a herman sonny blunt
earliest known earthly manifestation date: 22 may 1913 or 1914
bir
ming
ham

al
a
ma
bam
a
earthly transformation date: 30 may 1993
at his sisters house
bir
ming
ham

al
a
ma
bam
a

(continued)

6.

sun ra speaking
voice of the omniverse:

   "this is the song of tomorrows world
    you cant just play the notes
     you gotta feel the spirits
      4/4 time point 2
    fractions in rhythm harmony melody
     spirits dont need to count"

7.

listen i gotta go now cuz i dont want to be late for my gig in the omniverse
with sun ra & the myth science arkestra live! with me
the original urban bush woman infinitely spinning spinning
spinning the omniverse infinitely spinning the entrance
alone will last 2 centuries i am gonna do it like
this "from planet to planet" & like this & like
this traveling & then "from planet to planet"
traveling gonna gonna gonna "from
planet to planet"
"from planet to
planet"

SUN RA!

hattie gossett
performance poem for jawole
(See note on p. 141)

SUN RA

Ademola Olugebefola
mixed media
1994

THE CABINET OF DR. BUZZARD

Frank Smith

acrylic painting with collage on paper

1983

HOT RHYTHM

Archibald J. Motley, Jr.

oil on canvas

1961

The music. The music. Music is a moment. But life's a long time. In that moment, when it's good, when you really swinging—then you joined to everything, to everybody, to skies and stars and every living thing. But music ain't kissing. Kissing's what you want to do. Music's what you *got* to do, *if* you got to do it. Question is how long you can keep up with the music when you ain't got nobody to kiss. You know, the music don't come out of the air, baby. It comes out of the man who's blowing it.

from **THE AMEN CORNER**

James Baldwin

Bop began with jazz but one afternoon somewhere on a sidewalk maybe 1939, 1940, Dizzy Gillespie or Charley Parker or Thelonious Monk was walking down past a men's clothing store on 42nd Street or South Main in L.A. and from the loudspeaker they suddenly heard a wild impossible mistake in jazz that could only have been heard inside their own imaginary head, and that is a new art. Bop.

On the piano that night Thelonious introduced a wooden off-key note to everybody's warmup notes, Minton's Playhouse, evening starts, jam hours later, 10 P.M., colored bar and hotel next door, one or two white visitors some from Columbia some from Nowhere—some from ships—some from Army Navy Air Force Marines—some from Europe—The strange note makes the trumpeter of the band lift an eyebrow. Dizzy is surprised for the first time that day. He puts the trumpet to lips and blows a wet blur—

"Hee ha ha!" laughs Charley Parker bending down to slap his ankle. He puts his alto to his mouth and says "Didn't I tell you?"—with jazz of notes... Talking eloquent like great poets of foreign languages singing in foreign countries with lyres, by seas, and no one understands because the language isn't alive in the land yet—Bop is the language from America's inevitable Africa, *going* is sounded like *gong*, Africa is the name of the flue and kick beat, off to one side—the sudden squeak uninhibited that screams muffled at any moment from Dizzy Gillespie's trumpet—do anything you want—drawing the tune aside along another improvisation bridge with a reach-out tear of claws, why be subtle and false?

"Skidilibee-la-bee you,—oo,—e bop she bam, ske tooria—Parasakiliaoolza—menooriastibatiolyait—oon ya koo." They came into their own, they jumped, they had jazz and took it in their hands and saw its history vicissitudes and developments and turned it to their weighty use and heavily carried it clanking like posts across the enormity of a new world philosophy and a new strange and crazy grace came over them, fell from the air free, they saw pity in the hole of heaven, hell in their hearts, Billy Holliday had rocks in her heart, Lester droopy porkpied hung his horn and blew bop lazy ideas inside jazz had everybody dreaming (Miles Davis leaning against the piano fingering his trumpet with a cigarette hand working making raw iron sound like wood speaking in long sentences like Marcel Proust)— "Hey Jim," and the stud comes swinging down the street and says he's real *bent* and he's *down* and he has a *twisted* face, he works, he wails, he bops, he bangs, this man who was sent, stoned and stabbed is now *down*, *bent* and *stretched-out*— he is home at last, his music is here to stay, his history has washed over us, his imperialistic kingdoms are coming.

WE CAME TO PLAY

J. Michael Howard
acrylic on canvas
1992

from THE BEGINNING OF BOP

Jack Kerouac

ELLA FITZGERALD AND DIZZY GILLESPIE

William P. Gottlieb
photograph
1947

During the war years when apartments were scarce, as they still are, my wife and I found a place which was comfortable. In order to avoid any complaints about noise, I did all my practicing in a studio and refrained from any trumpet cadenzas in the evening. Three in the morning the doorbell rang, and I opened it as far as the latch chain permitted. There was Bird, horn in hand, and he says,

"Let me in, Diz, I've got it; you must hear this thing I've worked out."

I had been putting down Bird's solos on paper, which is something Bird never had the patience for himself.

"Not now," I said. "Later, man, tomorrow."

"No," Bird cried. "I won't remember it tomorrow; it's in my head now; let me in please."

From the other room, my wife yelled, "Throw him out," and I obediently slammed the door in Bird's face. Parker then took his horn to his mouth and played the tune in the hallway. I grabbed pencil and paper and took it down from the other side of the door.

from JAZZ ANECDOTES

Dizzy Gillespie
quoted by Bill Crow

GERRY MULLIGAN, ZOOT SIMS, MERCURY RECORDING STUDIO, NYC

Herman Leonard
photograph
1955

If you know in advance every note you're going to play and just the way you're going to play it, there's no need to have feelings. Like that, if you've got a feeling, you just can't use it; you can't even stay interested. Music like that, you could almost make a machine play it for you.

DEXTER GORDON

Jarvis Grant
silver print
1989

from TREAT IT GENTLE

Sidney Bechet

For the moment, the jazz is playing; there is no melody, only notes, a myriad of tiny jolts. They know no rest, an inflexible order gives birth to them and destroys them without even giving them time to recuperate and exist for themselves. They race, they press forward, they strike me a sharp blow in passing and are obliterated. I would like to hold them back, but I know if I succeeded in stopping one it would remain between my fingers only as a raffish languishing sound. I must accept their death; I must even *will* it. I know few impressions stronger or more harsh.

from NAUSEA

Jean-Paul Sartre

STREET MUSIC, JENKINS BAND

Norman Lewis
oil on canvas
1944

UNTITLED, NO. 29

Alexis De Boeck
oil pastel on paper
1987

He listened in silence to the records I had brought with me.

He listened while Tatum played "Rosetta" and "St. Louis Blues" and "Moonglow" and part of "Begin the Beguine," and then he abruptly lifted the needle from the player.

"Yes?" he said. "You wanted me to listen. I listened."

I took a deep breath. "I want to play like that," I said.

"Like what?"

"Like what you just heard."

"What *is* that?" he said.

"Jazz."

"Ah, yes. Jazz."

"It's what I want to play."

"What do you mean?" he said. "For fun? For amusement?"

"Mr. Passaro..."

"Well, I can see no real harm in it," he said, surprising me; I had expected a tantrum similar to the one I'd provoked with my request for "You Turned the Tables on Me." But Passaro actually chuckled, and then said, "In fact, the man has good technique. Has he had classical training?"

"I don't know anything about him."

"What is he playing in the bass clef? Tenths? They sound like tenths to me. And not *open* tenths, either. You may find the stretch difficult. Well, try it, I don't think it can hurt you."

"I've already tried it," I said.

"Ah? And can you reach those chords?"

"I have to stretch for them, you're right."

"Well, that won't hurt you. His arpeggios are very clean, too; he *must* have had classical training. I'm not familiar with all the chords he played in the twelve-bar piece. What were those chords?"

"I don't know."

"They seem to utilize many notes outside the mode. Well, no matter. If you want to fool around with this for your own amusement, I have no..."

"*All* the time, Mr. Passaro."

"Eh?"

"I want to play it *all* the time."

"What do you mean, *all* the time?"

"That's what I want to play."

The room went silent.

"Let me understand you," Passaro said.

"I want you to teach me to play the way he plays," I said. "Art Tattum. That's his name. That's how I want to play."

"Iggie, this is a bad joke," Passaro said, and chuckled again. "I'm a very patient man, you know that by now, we've been together for more than seven years, very patient. But this is a bad joke. Are you finished with it? If so, I'd like to..."

"Mr. Passaro, can you teach me to play what he's playing?"

"No," Passaro said, his voice suddenly sharp. "Of *course* not! What are you saying?"

"I don't want to play this way anymore."

"What way?"

"This way," I said, and my hands moved out to the keyboard, and I ran through the first four bars of a Chopin scherzo, and then abruptly pulled back my hands and quietly said, "That way, Mr. Passaro."

"*That* way," he said, "is the only way I teach."

"Well," I said.

His voice softened again. "What is it?" he asked gently, and sat beside me on the piano bench. "Ah, Iggie, I've been stupid. Forgive me. Your recent loss, your brother, I know the grief you must...forgive me, please. Go home. Please. I'll see you next Saturday, do the exercises I gave you, get your hands back in shape, have you practiced much, I'm sure you haven't. Come back next week. Forgive me for being inconsiderate. I get so involved sometimes, I...forgive me."

"Mr. Passaro," I said, "I don't want to come back next week unless you can teach me to play like Tattum."

I felt Passaro stiffen beside me. He was silent for several moments, and then he rose, and moved away from the bench and the piano, and began pacing the floor.

"No," he said. "I won't allow this to happen. No. No, Iggie, I'm sorry. No. You can't do this. I will not permit it.

(continued)

It's been too long. No. I've given you...I've invested...I've... no. Enough! You'll go home, you'll do your exercises, and next week we'll pick up again on the Moussorgsky. There's a lot to be done. They are already holding auditions for many of the prizes. If we..."

"Mr. Passaro, I don't..."

"Stop it!" he shouted. "Do you want to kill me? Stop it, *please*, stop saying this...these...please, Iggie."

"I don't care about prizes, Mr. Passaro. I don't want any prizes. I want to play like Tattum."

"Tattum, Tattum, *quello sfaccime, che c'importa* Tattum? He's a piano player; you're an *artist!* I made you an *artist!* You came to me with talent, and I took it, and shaped it, and put in your hands what's in my *own* hands. You're destroying me. Do you want to destroy me, Iggie?"

"No, Mr. Passaro, but..."

"I thought you loved music. I thought my own love for music..."

"I *do* love music!"

"Then stop talking about trash!"

"I'm sorry, Mr. Passaro."

He fell silent. When he spoke again, he had controlled his anger, and his voice was intimately low.

"Iggie," he said, "how many pupils do you think...how many do I have like you? How many do you think?"

"I'm sorry, Mr. Passaro..."

"One. In twenty years, *one*. I have no others like you. I've *never* had another like you, I may never have another as long as I live. I've never lied to you, Iggie. Never. I said you'd win prizes, and you will. I said you'd play in Carnegie Hall..."

"I don't want to play in Carnegie Hall."

And then he exploded.

He called me an ingrate, he called me a fool, he called me an immature child, he told me I was *truly* blind if I was ready to throw away a brilliant career as a concert pianist. He told me he was not mistaken about my future, he would not have lavished such attention on me if for a moment, for a *single* moment, he had thought he was mistaken. And for *what?* Were all those hours of patient instruction to be wasted? Did I think it was a simple matter to teach a blind person? He had given me more time and more energy than he'd given all his other pupils together, and now *this*. He reviled my decision, he spit upon my decision, he told me I would come to regret it, he promised I would be back on my knees begging him to teach me again, and he told me by then it would be too late, my repertoire would be gone, I would have squandered precious hours on the playing of trash, my opportunity will have vanished, my promise will have corroded, my future will have been flushed down the toilet like shit.

"So go!" he shouted. "Leave me! And good luck to you!"

It was a curse.

In the back room of my grandfather's tailor shop, I told him of my decision. He listened carefully. He was sixty-three years old, and he had been in this country for forty-two years, and I think he still found many of its ways baffling and incomprehensible.

He was pensively silent for a long time.

Perhaps he was thinking if only he had sent Luke to college, perhaps he was thinking if only he had allowed Tony to join the Air Corps, perhaps he was thinking that here in this America you could not expect the young to follow in the footsteps of their elders, you had to let them go, you had to let them run, you had to set them free.

In his broken English, he said, "Go play you jazza. And *buona fortuna*, Ignazio."

It was a blessing.

from **STREETS OF GOLD**

Evan Hunter
(continued from previous page)

He loiters.
                              Restaurant vendors
Weep, or out of them rolls a restless glee.
The Lonesome Blues, the Long-lost Blues, I Want A
Big Fat Mama. Down these sore avenues
Comes no Saint-Saëns, no piquant elusive Grieg,
And not Tchaikovsky's wayward eloquence
And not the shapely tender drift of Brahms.
But could he love them? Since a man must bring
To music what his mother spanked him for
When he was two: bits of forgotten hate,
Devotion: whether or not his mattress hurts:
The little dream his father humored: the thing
His sister did for money: what he ate
For breakfast—and for dinner twenty years
Ago last autumn: all his skipped desserts.

The pasts of his ancestors lean against
Him. Crowd him. Fog out his identity.
Hundreds of hungers mingle with his own,
Hundreds of voices advise so dexterously
He quite considers his reactions his,
Judges he walks most powerfully alone,
That everything is—simply what it is.

from **THE SUNDAYS OF SATIN LEGS SMITH**

Gwendolyn Brooks

TRANSCENDENT OF THE BLUES

William Tolliver
oil on canvas
1992

LESTER YOUNG AND J.C. HEARD, HARLEM

Milt Hinton

photograph

1958

JAZZ ON A SUMMER'S DAY

Tom Phillips

charcoal and pastel on paper

1977

Young men on the rooftops changed their tune; spit and fiddled with the mouthpiece for a while and when they put it back in and blew out their cheeks it was just like the light of that day, pure and steady and kind of kind. You would have thought everything had been forgiven the way they played. The clarinets had trouble because the brass was cut so fine, not lowdown the way they love to do it, but high and fine like a young girl singing by the side of a creek, passing the time, her ankles cold in the water. The young men with brass probably never saw such a girl, or such a creek, but they made her up that day. On the rooftops. Some on 254 where there is no protective railing; another at 131, the one with the apple-green water tank, and somebody right next to it, 133, where lard cans of tomato plants are kept, and a pallet for sleeping at night. To find coolness and a way to avoid mosquitoes unable to fly that high up or unwilling to leave the tender neck meat near the street lamps. So from Lenox to St. Nicholas and across 135th men playing out their maple-sugar hearts, tapping it from four-hundred-year-old trees and letting it run down the trunk, wasting it because they didn't have a bucket to hold it and didn't want one either. They just wanted to let it run that day, slow if it wished, or fast, but a free run down trees bursting to give it up.

That's the way the young men on brass sounded that day. Sure of themselves, sure they were holy, standing up there on the rooftops, facing each other at first, but when it was clear that they had beat the clarinets out, they turned their backs on them, lifted those horns straight up and joined the light just as pure and steady and kind of kind.

from JAZZ
Toni Morrison

What stopped me in my tracks was that it was an old song by the Savoy Sultans being played on a downtown street in the middle of the afternoon. It was strange enough to hear that but even stranger to hear this jumping tune being played by a flute and a tenor saxophone. There was an emptiness in hearing these wind instruments sing a cappella—without a rhythm section of piano, bass, and drums—that made me think about a Japanese instrument, the shakuhachi, playing traditional Japanese music. For a moment, I thought the setting and the instrumentation to be terribly inappropriate, but then I realized that jazz was just as fitting on a street corner as anywhere else. "Music," as Sonny Rollins once said, "is an open sky." And good jazz could be played on anything from an accordion to a kazoo.

The young boy had his eyes closed, and the veins in his neck were pronounced as he blew. He gave the impression of being an altar boy praying fervently to a very impersonal god. But the sound of the instrument was so unlike the grave boy; it was humorous, sparkling, refulgent, soaring. Some of the lines sounded like laughing paradiddles one would drum on a tabletop with one's fingertips. In a word, it was triumphant. One became totally unaware of the fact that the saxophone was being played with absolutely no accompaniment except the riffing flute. Most of the time, when one hears the saxophone played alone it sounds like someone practicing. A saxophone does not have the same solo capacities as a piano, a guitar, a violin, or even a flute. Yet the boy did not sound as if he were practicing. There was such a depth of lyricism in his playing that one almost wanted to dance before the beauty of the sound. Indeed, when the old head and the young boy started exchanging riff patterns in a call-and-response way, many in the crowd began to tap their toes and nod their heads. I thought I had heard that sound before; it was so old-fashioned. No one played like that anymore; it was out of style. But it surely felt good; these two men were outswinging that legendary Harlem dance band whose song they were playing. It all sounded as familiar as home.

from **THE SULTANS OF SWING**

Gerald Early

SLUM SONG

Hughie Lee-Smith
oil on canvas
1960

IN THE MEASURE OF EVERY PART

Moe Brooker
oil on canvas
1990

GIFT OF THE SPIRIT

Moe Brooker
silk screen
1987

We were walking round and round in the yard and I hear a woman singing—the voice come from high up, from one of the small barred windows. At first I don't believe it. Why should anybody sing here? Nobody want to sing in jail, nobody want to do anything. There's no reason, and you have no hope. I think I must be asleep, dreaming, but I'm awake all right and I see all the others are listening too. A nurse is with us that afternoon, not a policewoman. She stop and look up at the window.

It's a smoky kind of voice, and a bit rough sometimes, as if those old dark walls theyselves are complaining, because they see too much misery—too much. But it don't fall down and die in the courtyard; seems to me it could jump the gates of the jail easy and travel far, and nobody could stop it. I don't hear the words—only the music. She sing one verse and she begin another, then she break off sudden. Everybody starts walking again, and nobody says one word. But as we go in I ask the woman in front who was singing. "That's the Holloway song," she says. "Don't you know it yet? She was singing from the punishment cells, and she tell the girls cheerio never say die."

I get a room near Victoria where the landlady accept one pound in advance, and next day I find a job in the kitchen of a private hotel close by. But I don't stay there long. I hear of another job going in a big store—altering ladies' dresses and I get that. I lie and tell them I work in very expensive New York shop. I speak bold and smooth faced, and they never check up on me. I make a friend there—Clarice—very light coloured, very smart, she have a lot to do with the customers and she laugh at some of them behind their backs. But I say it's not their fault if the dress don't fit. Special dress for one person only—that's very expensive in London. So it's take in, or let out all the time. Clarice have two rooms not far from the store. She furnish herself gradual and she gives parties sometimes Saturday nights. It's there I start whistling the Holloway Song. A man comes up to me and says, "Let's hear that again." So I whistle it again (I never sing now) and he tells me "Not bad." Clarice have an old piano somebody give her to store and he plays the tune, jazzing it up. I say, "No, not like that," but everybody else say the way he do it is first class. Well I think no more of this till I get a letter from him telling me he has sold the song and as I was quite a help he encloses five pounds with thanks.

I read the letter and I could cry. For after all, that song was all I had. I don't belong nowhere really, and I haven't money to buy my way to belonging. I don't want to either.

But when that girl sing, she sing to me and she sing for me. I was there because I was *meant* to be there. It was *meant* I should hear it—this I *know*.

Now I've let them play it wrong, and it will go from me like all the other songs—like everything. Nothing left for me at all.

But then I tell myself all this is foolishness. Even if they played it on trumpets, even if they played it just right, like I wanted—no walls would fall so soon. "So let them call it jazz," I think, and let them play it wrong. That won't make no difference to the song I heard.

I buy myself a dusty pink dress with the money.

from LET THEM CALL IT JAZZ

Jean Rhys

(for Louis Armstrong)

Louis i'm trying to understand what you were
here
how you left this place
how you gave the people bravura music
how you could survive it all
even bucket-a-blood
where the frustration of our people
                        boiled into daily slaughter
but then New O is an old place for that:

don't you think it's a moon-town
where the imagination of violence
sparks easily to life?
what festers in the minds
of the grandchildren of the
people you knew who languish
now in the projects?
bucket-a-blood was demolished
its people banished to the project
your old town
the city's new progress
your old house
gone for the city's new jailhouse
such the way it is the city
tells you what they think of you
& everyone like you & still the
people dance & progress looks on afraid...

Louis i'm trying to understand what you were
really like
in the dark moments away from the stage.
rumors have it you were not pleasant
to be around,
the shit-eating grin nowhere to be found:

did the moon-blood intrude
the sleep of your nights
even sleep of your days

did you carry moon-blood
memories to the grave?

Louis i'm trying to understand but never
mind
it's enough that you said don't bury me in
New Orleans
& it's enough to hear your trumpet
laughing at it all
it's enough that you played de-truth-de-truth-beeeeeeeee

& the sweaty handkerchief
honest enough   honest
it's enough
it's enough
but Lou/est

someday the dancers will explode
and all this little history
will shatter as the
shit-eating masks fall...
& only the moon will understand

Lou/is.

FOR LIL LOUIS

Tom Dent

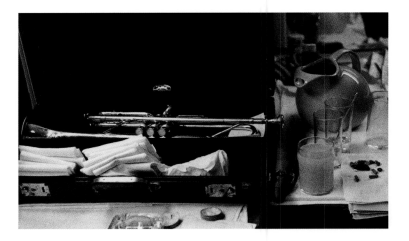

STILL LIFE (LOUIS ARMSTRONG'S HORN CASE)

Dennis Stock
photograph
1958

The very first thing I remember in my early childhood is a flame, a blue flame jumping off a gas stove somebody lit. It might have

been me playing around with the stove. I don't remember who it was. Anyway, I remember being shocked by the whoosh of the blue flame jumping off the burner, the suddenness of it. That's as far back as I can remember; any further back than this is just fog, you know, just mystery. But that stove flame is as clear as music is in my mind. I was three years old.

I saw that flame and felt that hotness of it close to my face. I felt fear, real fear, for the first time in my life. But I remember it also like some kind of adventure, some kind of weird joy, too.

I guess that experience took me someplace in my head I hadn't been before. To some frontier, the edge, maybe, of everything possible. I don't know; I never tried to analyze it before. The fear I had was almost like an invitation, a challenge to go forward into something I knew nothing about. That's where I think my personal philosophy of life and my commitment to everything I believe in started, with that moment.

MAGUS MANTIS

Randall Schmit
oil, acrylic, pastel, and graphite on canvas
1989

from MILES: THE AUTOBIOGRAPHY

Miles Davis

AFRICAN JAZZ #1

Michael Cummings
quilt
1990

AFRICAN JAZZ #4

Michael Cummings
quilt
1990

AFRICAN JAZZ #11

Michael Cummings
quilt
1990

AFRICAN JAZZ #12

Michael Cummings
quilt
1990

A tall, dark, bearish, inward-shining man, he wore odd hats and dark glasses with bamboo frames when he played. His body moved continuously. At the keyboard, he swayed back and forth and from side to side, his feet flapping like flounders on the floor. While his sidemen soloed, he stood by the piano and danced, turning in slow, genial circles, his elbows out like wings, his knees slightly bent, his fingers snapping on the after-beat. His motions celebrated what he and his musicians played: Watch, these are the shapes of my music.

I'D RATHER BE SHARP THAN A B FLAT

Jean Perschbacher Fujio
fiber
1993

from GOODBYES AND OTHER MESSAGES

Whitney Balliett
on Thelonious Monk

UNTITLED (OFFICE WALL, VILLAGE VANGUARD)

Anthony Barboza
photograph
1988

like Thelonious Monk

I record my love for you
and no one understands it

the complexity of my
declarations

the strange way
it makes you feel

ASK ME NOW

E. Ethelbert Miller

THE GIFT OF PRESENCE

Raymond Saunders
mixed media on wood
1993-94

CALL & RESPONSE

Call and response refers to the Sunday service: "Say 'Amen' somebody"—"AMEN!" This interaction between preachers and congregations all over black America has become an integral feature of cultural expression in the United States. Born in West and Central Africa, where one experiences it in exchanges among singers and instrumentalists (as well as dancers and sculptors), in the U.S. this pattern occurs in church songs and sermons and also in work songs, play songs (such as "Little Sally Walker"), blues, rags, and in jazz. You say something; I say something back.

Call and response in jazz may consist of a two-part song within the single self—a dialogue between the pianist's right hand and the left; an instrumentalist/singer's exchange between the voice and the accompanying *box* or *axe.*

Jazz call and response also identifies complicated exchanges between a single voice and other voices: soloist and the chorus of other players; soloist and the congregation of listeners and dancers. These conversations in the language of jazz may be friendly or exhortative in the mode of the preacher and the amening congregation. They may be mutual praise songs or friendly games of leap frog.

They may also involve knock-down competitions, challenges, games of innuendo, ritual insult, mockery. Sometimes signifying contests (also called "cutting contests") involve big-mouthing and virtuoso sounding off. Dizzy Gillespie and Roy Eldridge were fearsome cutting contestants because, while they loved to whisper and pray through their horns, they also knew how to lie, wrangle, cuss an opponent down and, if need be, out. Call and response could be sweet, call and response could be rough.

It is a fascinating phenomenon that the call and response circle in jazz often widens to include dancers and listeners who are not dancing, but whose rapt attention and well-timed foot tapping become part of the total performance. In our (post-) modern world, jazz listeners respond to musicians' calls sent by radio or record (and C.D.) players. The hearer's response to jazz music may be to think things over yet again; the response may be to push back the furniture and dance or to turn the lights down low and have a very private party. Like jazz improvisors who transform every composition they play, listeners add their own sweet or bitter notes to the music and make it their own.

To the jazz musician, the "call" of jazz may come from an almost indescribably subtle attitude of a dancer. It may come from the example of Louis Armstrong, sounding like a century-full of music buzz-toned through the barrel of a single magic horn.

Visual and literary artists are parties to this dynamic process of jazz calling and responding. For not only do they respond to the work of people in their own fields (novelist Ellison to novelist Dostoevski, muralist James Phillips to the muralists of Mexico), they also call and respond to jazz music and its makers. This book's sections on rhythm and improvisation tell part of the story of how this process works. A jazz rhythm by Max Roach (a call) becomes a rhythm of color in a Roland Jean collage (a response); an improvisation by Charlie Parker becomes an improvised line in a Norman Lewis sketch. Writers hear the call of the music and respond with words that swing and chapters that take a jazz shape. Call, countercall; call, recall; call, response.

Perhaps above all, these writers and visual artists respond to jazz music's beautiful call for unequivocal excellence. "If I could write a poem as perfect as Parker's solo or paint a picture as evocative as Ellington's 'Mood Indigo,'" these works seem to say, "well then maybe, wherever they are, Bird and Duke would respond to me across the distances of space and time, would give to me a full-throated, full-spirited *amen.*" *Robert O'Meally*

JAZZ VILLAGE

Romare Bearden
mixed media and collage on board
1967

Swing, bebop, cool, a counterpoint of romanticism and classicism, hot and intellectual jazz, human music, music with a history in contrast to stupid animal dance music, the polka, the waltz, the *zamba*, a music that could be known and liked in Copenhagen as well as in Mendoza or Capetown, a music that brings adolescents together, with records under their arms, that gives them names and melodies to use as passwords so they can know each other and become intimate and feel less lonely surrounded by bosses, families, and bitter love affairs, a music that accepts all imaginations and tastes, a collection of instrumental 78's with Freddie Keppard or Bunk Johnson, the reactionary cult of Dixieland, an academic specialization in Bix Beiderbecke, or in the adventures of Thelonious Monk, Horace Silver, or Thad Jones, the vulgarities of Erroll Garner or Art Tatum, repentance and rejection, a preference for small groups, mysterious recordings with false names and strange titles and labels made up on the spur of the moment, and that whole freemasonry of Saturday nights in a student's room or in some basement café with girls who would rather dance to *Stardust* or *When Your Man Is Going to Put You Down*, and have a sweet slow smell of perfume and skin and heat, and let themselves be kissed when the hour is late and somebody has put on *The Blues with a Feeling* and hardly anybody is really dancing, just standing up together, swaying back and forth, and everything is hazy and dirty and lowdown and every man is in a mood to tear off those warm girdles as his hands go stroking shoulders and the girls have their mouths half-opened and turn themselves over to delightful fear and the night, while a trumpet comes on to possess them in the name of all men, taking them with a single hot phrase that drops them like a cut flower into the arms of their partners, and there comes a motionless race, a jump up into the night air, over the city, until a miniature piano brings them to again, exhausted, reconciled, and still virgins until next Saturday, all of this from a kind of music that horrifies solid citizens who think that nothing is true unless there are programs and ushers, and that's the way things are and jazz is like a bird who migrates or emigrates or immigrates or transmigrates, roadblock jumper, smuggler, something that runs and mixes in and tonight in Vienna Ella Fitzgerald is singing while in Paris Kenny Clarke is helping open a new *cave* and in Perpignan Oscar Peterson's fingers are dancing around and Satchmo, everywhere, with that gift of omnipresence given him by the Lord, in Birmingham, in Warsaw, Milan, in Buenos Aires, in Geneva, in the whole world, is inevitable, is rain and bread and salt, something completely beyond national ritual, sacred traditions, language and folklore: a cloud without frontiers, a spy of air and water, an archetypal form, something from before, from below, that brings Mexicans together with Norwegians and Russians and Spaniards, brings them back into that obscure and forgotten central flame, clumsily and badly and precariously he delivers them back to a betrayed origin, he shows them that perhaps there have been other paths and that the one they took was maybe not the only one or the best one, or that perhaps there have been other paths and that the one they took was the best, but that perhaps there were other paths that made for softer walking and that they had not taken those, or that they only took them in a halfway sort of way, and that a man is always more than a man and always less than a man, more a man because he has in himself all that jazz suggests and lies in wait for and even anticipates, and less than a man because he has made an aesthetic and sterile game out of this liberty, a chessboard where one must be bishop or knight, a definition of liberty which is taught in school, in the very schools where the pupils are never taught ragtime rhythm or the first notes of the blues, and so forth and so on.

from HOPSCOTCH

Julio Cortazar

MONA LISA

Roland Jean
mixed media on board
1985

the ceremonies were over

curious festivities where

I pay to see and be seen

the audience entertains the artists

verushka looks great in that fur

shut up is plastic

harper's bazaar is flown to me every month

otherwise I look at the stands in copenhagen

meanwhile roy

who couldn't share the fun

went underground

basement shelter friends piano drinks dim lights

undid tie loosened shirt

inhaled inhaled inhaled

filled his diaphragm with love

and blew his first endlesssssssssssssssssssssssssss note

UNTITLED (MUSICIANS ON DECK)

Anthony Barboza

photograph

1983

ROY ELDRIDGE

Hermenegildo Sábat

GENE AMMONS/ARCHIE SHEPP

Archie Rand
acrylic resin and mixed media on canvas
1970

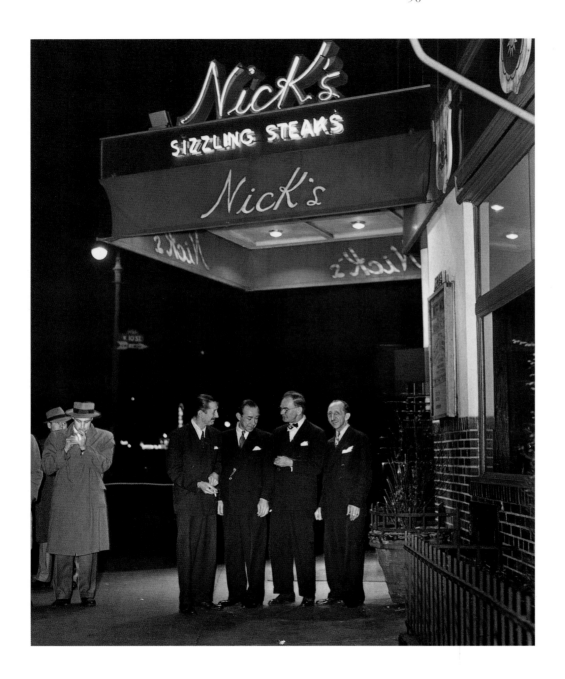

NICK'S (Pee Wee Russell, Muggsy Spanier, Miff Mole, Joe Grauso)

William P. Gottlieb

photograph

1946

I crisscrossed with Monk
Wailed with Bud
Counted every star with Stitt
Sang "Don't Blame Me" with Sarah
Wore a flower like Billie
Screamed in the range of Dinah
& scatted "How High The Moon" with Ella Fitzgerald
as she blew roof off the Shrine Auditorium
                              Jazz at the Philharmonic

I cut my hair into a permanent tam
Made my feet rebellious metronomes
Embedded record needles in paint on paper
Talked bopology talk
Laughed in high pitched saxophone phrases
Became keeper of every Bird riff
every Lester lick
as Hawk melodicized my ear of infatuated tongues
& Blakey drummed militant messages in
soul of my applauding teeth
& Ray hit bass notes to the last love seat in my bones
I moved in triple time with Max
Grooved high with Diz
Perdidoed with Pettiford
Flew home with Hamp
Shuffled in Dexter's Deck
Squatty rooed with Peterson
Dreamed a "52nd Street Theme" with Fats
& scatted "Lady Be Good" with Ella Fitzgerald
as she blew roof off the Shrine Auditorium
Jazz at the Philharmonic

JAZZ FAN LOOKS BACK

Jayne Cortez

MINTON'S (Thelonious Monk, Howard McGhee, Roy Eldridge, Teddy Hill)

William P. Gottlieb
photograph
1946

music is your mistress;
demanding constant love
and international settings.

as always, you stroll beside her.

aging, grumpy orchestra
springs into elegance at the drop
of your hand.

even so, there are casualties.

the years pass,
you bury rabbit and swee'pea,
run your fingers across the black keys,
dip the color in your hair.

cancerous nodes
rush toward a harrowing cadenza,
pen kisses paper.

a lover
in no particular hurry,
the music reveals itself
a negligee black note at a time.

FOR DUKE ELLINGTON

Reuben Jackson

DUKE ELLINGTON AND BENNY GOODMAN LISTEN TO ELLA FITZGERALD

Herman Leonard
photograph
1949

UNTITLED (DIGITIZED SECTION OF DUKE ELLINGTON)

Robert Graham

wax

1988

what did Ellington mean
when he said

"I love you madly"

his hands touching a
piano not made of flesh

DO NOTHIN' TILL YOU HEAR FROM ME
E. Ethelbert Miller

BLUE LIGHT (FOR DUKE ELLINGTON)
Douglas Vogel
mixed media with electric light
1981-82

From a pocket Billy had taken out a matchbook. A few chord progressions had been scribbled on the inside cover. Then, drawing out a small lined tablet from beneath the seat, he quickly drew a bass staff and started humming.

"You got something going?" Earl asked.

"I think, yeah. A little light something, you know, like bright light and spring-time and whatnot."

Earl tapped the wheel lightly with the palm of his free hand. "Toss in a small woman's bouncy walk, and I might get excited with you."

"Well, help me then. This time you use the woman—tight yellow skirt, right?—and I'll use the light, the light of mid-May, and when they don't work together, I think we'll both know."

"Solid. What you got so far?"

Billy did not answer. He kept a finger to his ear, staring from the matchbook cover to the tablet. Earl let it run. You don't interrupt when the idea is so young.

More often than not, Billy and Earl brought opposites or, at least, unlikely combinations together. One of the band's more popular numbers, a blues, was the result of Billy's meditations on the richly perfumed arms of a large and fleshy woman, arms tightly holding a man who mistook her short laugh for joy. To this, Earl had brought the memory of a rainy night and a long soft moan carried on the wind, something heard from the end of an alley. They used only the colors and sounds from these images, and only later, when the songs were fully arranged, did the smell and the touch of them sweep in. There had been other songs that resolved the contrasts, the differences, between the drone of a distant train and an empty glass of gin, a lipstick print at its rim, fingerprints around it. A baby's whimpering, and a man grinning as he counted a night's big take from the poker table, painted bright red fingernails tapping lightly down a lover's arm, and the cold of a lonely apartment. How much did the dancing couples, those whispering and holding close as second skins or those bouncing and whirling tirelessly, feel these things, too? Or did they bring something entirely different to the rhythms, something of their own?

from LUSH LIFE

John McCluskey, Jr.

DANCING COUPLE NO. 2

Ann Tanksley
oil on canvas
1992

THE LINDY HOP

Miguel Covarrubias
lithograph
1936

We began at The Silver Shadow
Doing the Hully Gully,
Till we were dizzy with the scent
Of perfume on our hands. The jukebox
Blazed a path across the semi-dark
Dancefloor as we moved like swimmers
Against each other. April burned
Into the night, after the teenage club
Was padlocked & the scarred WWII
Vets who chaperoned went home
To wives. Some cars nosed into
Backwood lanes as wine bottles
Passed from hand to hand, girls
In their laps, but we sped off
Toward Dead Man's Curve
On two wheels, headed for The Plantation
Club slouched a half mile
Back into fragrant pines.
Off-duty deputy sheriffs guarded doors,
Protecting crap tables in the back room.
The place smelled of catfish & rotgut. "Honey Hush"
Pulled us into its pulsebeat,
& somehow I had the prettiest woman
In the room. Her dress whirled
A surge of blue, & my butterfly-toes
Were copacetic & demonic.

Creame-colored leather
& black suede—my lucky shoes—
I could spin on those radiant heels,
No longer in that country town.
She'd loop out till our fingertips
Touched & then was back in my arms;
The hem of her dress snapped
Like a boy's shoeshine rag.
She was a woman who would take her time,
Unlike the girls an hour earlier.
We were hot colors rushing toward
the darkest corner, about to kiss,
When some joker cut in
& pulled her into his arms.
I was still swept onward by the timbre
Of her breath, her body,
As I moved to the jangle of three
Silver dollars my grandfather gave me
Five years earlier. I didn't see
The flash when her husband burst in.
Someone knocked the back door off its hinges,
& for a moment the shuffle of feet
Were on the deck of a Dutch Man of War.
I'm still backing away
From the scene, a scintilla
Of love & murder.

BUTTERFLY-TOED SHOES

Yusef Komunyakaa

TOSHIKO

Mahler Ryder
wood and acrylic paint
1990

some springs the mississippi rose up so high
it drowned the sound of singing and escape
that sound of jazz from back
boarded shanties by railroad tracks
visionary women letting pigeons loose
on unsettled skies
was drowned by the quiet ballad of natural disaster
some springs song was sweeter even so
sudden cracks split the sky/ for only a second
lighting us in a kind of laughter
as we rolled around quilted histories
extended our arms and cries to the rain
that kept us soft together

some springs the mississippi rose up so high
it drowned the sound of singing and escape
church sisters prayed and rinsed
the brown dinge tinting linens
thanked the trees for breeze
and the greenness sticking to the windows
the sound of jazz from back
boarded shanties by railroad tracks
visionary women letting pigeons loose
on unsettled skies
some springs song was sweeter even so

C.T.'S VARIATION

Thulani Davis

ON THE ROAD

Vincent D. Smith

monotype

1989

At Odd Fellows Hall: Nobody took their hats off. It was plenty rough. You paid fifteen cents and walked in. The band, six of them was sitting on a low stand. They had their hats on and were resting, pretty sleepy. All of a sudden, Buddy stomps, knocks on the floor with his trumpet to give the beat and they all sit up straight.

UNTITLED (MUSICIAN'S FEET WITH MUTES)

Gordon Parks
photograph
1960

from BAQUET ON BOLDEN

George Baquet

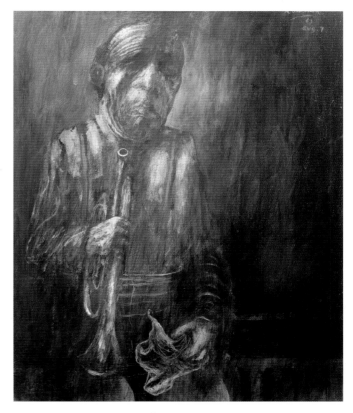

PRESERVATION HALL

David Ellis
india ink on paper
1993

MEMORY OF PUNCH MILLER

Noel Rockmore
oil on masonite
1963

It was late in the afternoon now. Bessie Smith was on the phonograph, so that meant that Sugar Mecklin's daddy was already drunk. Sugar Mecklin's daddy called his Bessie Smith records his wrist-cutting music. It was Bessie Smith singing a long time ago when Gilbert Mecklin stuck the ice pick in his chest. *my mama says I'm reckless* Bessie Smith had sung that day, and he knew just what she meant too, he was reckless too. *my daddy says I'm wild* Bessie Smith sang. Nobody knew better than Gilbert Mecklin what it meant to be reckless and wild. Nobody in this world. *I ain't good looking* she sang *but I'm somebody's angel child* Bessie Smith had been singing that day before Sugar Mecklin was even born. In a way that was the good old days, Gilbert Mecklin remembered them fondly, that day long time ago when he had let the record play to its end and then jammed an ice pick straight into his breast bone.

Sugar Mecklin had heard all about it, and he couldn't help wishing that Bessie Smith was not on the phonograph on this particular day. He wished instead that his daddy had waited until after Sugar had had time to come home and say, "Me and Sweet found a dead man. Can Sweet sleep over tonight?" before he started playing wrist-cutting music.

And, if the truth be knew—this was a phrase that Gilbert Mecklin used and drove Sugar's mama straight out of her last and only mind, "if the truth be knew"—Gilbert Mecklin was just this minute saying to himself, he his ownself would have preferred not to be drunk this afternoon. If the truth be knew, Gilbert Mecklin was sitting there in his chair thinking, Now I wonder how this happened again, just when I didn't want it to happen, how did it come to pass that I am sitting here unintentionally drunk on my ass with wrist-cutting music playing on the record player when I have great need to comfort two children who have lost so much and seen too much death in their little lives? The alcohol made Gilbert Mecklin groggy. He felt a little like he had been hit over the head and covered with a heavy blanket.

On the phonograph now there was a trombone. It started way down low, and it could have been the voice of a Texas longhorn cow at first, or an alligator in a swamp quartet singing bass, it was so low. Gilbert Mecklin listened to it. He had to. Nobody else knew how to listen to it. His wife sure hell didn't know how to listen to music. She didn't appreciate music. The trombone note was rising now, rising up and up. Listen to that clear note rise up from the muddy waters of the Delta!

from MUSIC OF THE SWAMP

Lewis Nordan

Because there was a man somewhere in a candystripe silk shirt,

gracile and dangerous as a jaguar and because a woman moaned

for him in sixty-watt gloom and mourned him Faithless Love

Twotiming Love Oh Love Oh Careless Aggravating Love,

She came out on the stage in yards of pearls, emerging like

a favorite scenic view, flashed her golden smile and sang.

Because grey laths began somewhere to show from underneath

torn hurdygurdy lithographs of dollfaced heaven;

and because there were those who feared alarming fists of snow

on the door and those who feared the riot-squad of statistics,

She came out on the stage in ostrich feathers, beaded satin,

and shone that smile on us and sang.

BESSIE SMITH

Morgan Monceaux
mixed media
1993

HOMAGE TO THE EMPRESS OF THE BLUES

Robert Hayden

HARLEM JAZZ JAMBOREE

Norman Lewis
oil on canvas
1943

Back in 1937, Jelly Roll Morton was part owner of a sleazy night club upstairs from a U Street hamburger stand in Washington, D.C. At the time, I was finishing high school and playing gigs around the city as often as they came my way. I was a good, proud, seventeen years old then, and quite naturally very little remained which I did not know about life and music. I used to hang around with several other young pianists, kids like myself who were starting to study their Hindemith and Bartók and Schönberg and Webern; we also knew our jazz. Of course, *our* jazz began with Art Tatum and Prez, and obviously there was no place in it for old men like Mr. Morton. We had never even bothered to listen to him.

But when we heard that Jelly had this little club in Washington—I think it was called the Jungle Inn—we decided to take a ride down and have a few laughs. Even though it was a Saturday night we had no trouble getting a booth in the place. Somebody recognized us as part of the new crop of jazz pianists; word started to pass around the house that some young hipsters had stopped in to have some fun with old Jelly Roll.

And then Jelly came on. He looked shockingly sick and feeble—old and a little mad. But he wore his old, southern-gentleman's suit with dignity, and when he smiled the diamond in his tooth still glittered hard. He played a new piece of his called *Sweet Substitute*, and then (since the grapevine grows quick in little places like this) he looked straight over at our booth. His eyes had a very personal kind of pride which I had never seen before. His look had the strangely arrogant wisdom of those who know, those who have been there and seen it and at the end realized that nothing very shattering has happened after all. Dying is a slow and shabby business.

Then Jelly spoke only to us: "You punks can't play this."

I forget the tune. What I do remember is a big, full, two-handed piano player—a ragtimer modified and relaxed by way of New Orleans, and *very* swinging. I suppose the tune was corny, now that I look back on it, but it had a charm of its own. There was something extremely personal about it which defied description; and as I listened suddenly I knew. "Golly, he's right. I *can't* play what he's playing. Just purely technically I can't play two hands together and separately the way he does." I looked over at the other confident young men who had come with me; I saw that they knew they couldn't either. Ours was a very quiet booth for the next three hours.

from THE LOST GENERATION

Billy Taylor

I used to visit all the very gay places,

Those come what may places

Where one relaxes on the axis

Of the wheel of life

To get the feel of life

from jazz and cocktails.

The girls I knew had sad and sullen gray faces

With distingué traces

That used to be there, you could see where

They'd been washed away

By too many through the day

Twelve o'clock tales.

Then you came along with your siren song

To tempt me to madness.

I thought for a while that your poignant smile

Was tinged with the sadness of a great love for me.

Ah, yes, I was wrong,

Again I was wrong.

Life is lonely again

And only last year

Everything seemed so sure.

Now life is awful again,

A trough full of heart

Could only be a bore.

A week in Paris will ease the bite of it.

All I care is to smile in spite of it.

I'll forget you, I will

While yet you are still

Burning inside my brain.

Romance is mush

Stifling those who strive.

I'll live a lush life in some small dive

And there I'll be while I rot with the rest

Of those whose lives are lonely, too.

LUSH LIFE

Billy Strayhorn

CAFE L'AVENUE

Palmer Hayden
watercolor and graphite on paper
1932

He left soon after dinner, but not to go home. He was curious to see Paris by night with clearer and more judicious eyes than those of other days. He bought a *strapontin* for the Casino and watched Josephine Baker go through her chocolate arabesques.

After an hour he left and strolled toward Montmartre, up the Rue Pigalle into the Place Blanche. The rain had stopped and there were a few people in evening clothes disembarking from taxis in front of cabarets, and *cocottes* prowling singly or in pairs, and many Negroes. He passed a lighted door from which issued music, and stopped with the sense of familiarity; it was Bricktop's, where he had parted with so many hours and so much money. A few doors farther on he found another ancient rendezvous and incautiously put his head inside. Immediately an eager orchestra burst into sound, a pair of professional dancers leaped to their feet and a maître d'hôtel swooped toward him, crying, "Crowd just arriving, sir!" But he withdrew quickly.

"You have to be damn drunk," he thought.

Zelli's was closed, the bleak and sinister cheap hotels surrounding it were dark; up in the Rue Blanche there was more light and a local, colloquial French crowd. The Poet's Cave had disappeared, but the two great mouths of the Café of Heaven and the Café of Hell still yawned—even devoured, as he watched, the meager contents of a tourist bus—a German, a Japanese, and an American couple who glanced at him with frightened eyes.

So much for the effort and ingenuity of Montmartre. All the catering to vice and waste was on an utterly childish scale, and he suddenly realized the meaning of the word "dissipate"—to dissipate into thin air; to make nothing out of something. In the little hours of the night every move from place to place was an enormous human jump, an increase of paying for the privilege of slower and slower motion.

He remembered thousand-franc notes given to an orchestra for playing a single number, hundred-franc notes tossed to a doorman for calling a cab.

But it hadn't been given for nothing.

It had been given, even the most wildly squandered sum, as an offering to destiny that he might not remember the things most worth remembering, the things that now he would always remember—his child taken from his control, his wife escaped to a grave in Vermont.

In the glare of a *brasserie* a woman spoke to him. He bought her some eggs and coffee, and then, eluding her encouraging stare, gave her a twenty-franc note and took a taxi to his hotel.

from **BABYLON REVISITED**

F. Scott Fitzgerald

NEGRO JAZZ BAND

Charles Demuth
watercolor on paper
1916

ESPERANDO UN POCO (WAITING A LITTLE)

Juan Alberto Garcia de Cubas
collage with watercolor, pencil, ink, and photocopy

1993

Alone,

not blue,

just alone.

    Big room,
    hi fi, t.v.,
    drink and
    cigarette

Alone,

not blue,

just alone.

    Waiting . . .

NOT BLUE

Hattie M. Cumbo

AFTER FIESTA, REMORSE, SIESTA

Archibald J. Motley, Jr.
oil on canvas
1959-60

So I went on up there one Sunday and went on across the boulevard, and I looked around and there was Street's hotel on the corner, a big, fine, beautiful hotel. At Eighteenth and Vine there was a pool hall, a barbershop, the Subway Club downstairs in the same block as the barbershop. I said to myself, "Well, looka here, this is it." There was also a big barbecue stand in the next block. So I kept on walking, and further up Eighteenth Street there was a little dime-movie place. So I went in there, and they had a piano that had all kinds of sound effects on it to go with the silent pictures. It even had the sound for horses' hooves for the cowboy pictures. Naturally I was very interested in that.

I didn't get any farther up Eighteenth Street than that dime-movie place that first time. But when I took another walk up there the next week, I made a turn on Vine Street, and that's when I came to the Eblon. It was a little movie theater, and there was a special little sign announcing that they had just recently installed a Wicks organ, a manual Wicks, which hadn't been in there more than two or three weeks, I guess.

So I happened to have twenty-five or thirty cents in my pocket, and I used one of my treasured dimes for admission and went in and sat down front as I always did when there was an organ in the theater. There was a woman in there playing the organ while the picture was on. Then at the end of the main feature there was a seven-piece band that came on and played for the cartoons and short subjects. The leader was a violin player called Gooby Taylor, and the drummer was Baby Lovett, one of the local musicians I had met in some joint before going in the hospital. When they finished, they went out into the alley, and I went out and joined them, and Baby and I got to talking, and I said I saw you up on Twelfth Street, and we talked on and talked on. And I said I'd like to play that organ in there.

"What you mean?" he said giving me a funny glance.

"I'd like to play it," I told him. "I can play that thing."

He knew that I was a piano player because he had heard me sitting in at one of the joints. But he didn't know I could play organ too. He said something about the woman coming back and telling Gooby, but I kept on after him.

"Do you know how to turn it on?"

"Yeah," he said, "I know how to turn it on."

"Well, turn it on."

But he just looked at me. "You're sure you know what you're doing?"

"Shit yeah, man," I said. "I can turn it on myself. All you got to do is put that switch on back there."

"Look, you going make me lose my job," he said, and then he said, "Go ahead, but if anything happens, I don't know you. Hell, I don't even know how you got down there."

The woman still wasn't back from wherever she went for lunch or whatever she went out to do, and the feature picture was back on again. So I finally got him to go back there and turn the switch on, and I went in and started. There was a sad scene up on the screen. The audience really should have been just about ready to cry. But I opened up with the "Bugle Blues" on the organ, and the kids in there for the matinee started clapping right after I hit the break. Two or three of them breaks and the house was rocking.

from GOOD MORNING BLUES

Count Basie

In the old days the voice was high and clear and poignantly lyrical. Steel-bright in its upper range and, at its best, silky smooth, it was possessed of a purity somehow impervious to both the stress of singing above a twelve-piece band and the urgency of Rushing's own blazing fervor. On dance nights, when you stood on the rise of the school grounds two blocks to the east, you could hear it jetting from the dance hall like a blue flame in the dark; now soaring high above the trumpets and trombones, now skimming the froth of reeds and rhythm as it called some woman's anguished name—or demanded in a high, thin, passionately lyrical line, "Baaaaay-bay, Bay-aaaay-bay! Tell me what's the matter now!"—above the shouting of the swinging band.

BASIE AT THE APOLLO
Wadsworth Jarrell
acrylic on canvas
1992

from SOUND AND THE MAINSTREAM
Ralph Ellison

JAZZ MUSICIANS

Nobou Nakamura

photograph

1983

I am a cowboy in the boat of Ra,
sidewinders in the saloons of fools
bit my forehead   like   O
the untrustworthiness of Egyptologists
who do not know their trips. Who was that
dog-faced man? they asked, the day I rode
from town.

School marms with halitosis cannot see
the Nefertiti fake chipped on the run by slick
germans, the hawk behind Sonny Rollins' head or
the ritual beard of his axe; a longhorn winding
its bells thru the Field of Reeds.

I am a cowboy in the boat of Ra. I bedded
down with Isis, Lady of the Boogaloo, dove
down deep in her horny, stuck up her Wells-Far-ago
in daring midday getaway. 'Start grabbing the
blue,' I said from top of my double crown.

I am a cowboy in the boat of Ra. Ezzard Charles
of the Chisholm Trail. Took up the bass but they
blew off my thumb. Alchemist in ringmanship but a
sucker for the right cross.

I am a cowboy in the boat of Ra. Vamoosed from
the temple i bide my time. The price on the wanted
poster was a-going down, outlaw alias copped my stance
and moody greenhorns were making me dance;
            while my mouth's
shooting iron got its chambers jammed.

I am a cowboy in the boat of Ra. Boning-up in
the ol West i bide my time. You should see
me pick off these tin cans whippersnappers. I
write the motown long plays for the comeback of
Osiris. Make them up when stars stare at sleeping
steer out here near the campfire. Women arrive
on the backs of goats and throw themselves on
my Bowie.

I am a cowboy in the boat of Ra. Lord of the lash,
the Loup Garou Kid. Half breed son of Pisces and
Aquarius. I hold the souls of men in my pot. I do
the dirty boogie with scorpions. I make the bulls
keep still and was the first swinger to grape the taste.

I am a cowboy in his boat. Pope Joan of the
Ptah Ra. C/mere a minute willya doll?
Be a good girl and
bring me my Buffalo horn of black powder
bring me my headdress of black feathers
bring me my bones of Ju-Ju snake
go get my eyelids of red paint.
Hand me my shadow

I'm going into town after Set

I am a cowboy in the boat of Ra

look out Set   here I come Set
to get Set   to sunset Set
to unseat Set   to Set down Set

      usurper of the Royal couch
      —imposter RAdio of Moses' bush
      party pooper O hater of dance
      vampire outlaw of the milky way

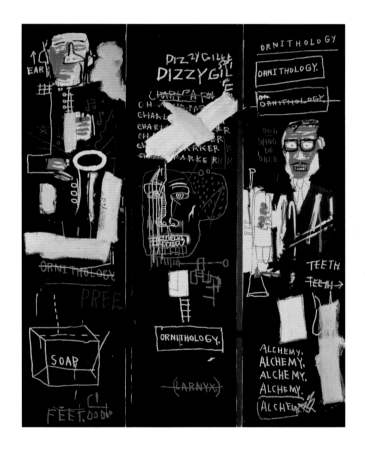

I AM A COWBOY IN THE BOAT OF RA

Ishmael Reed

HORN PLAYERS

Jean-Michel Basquiat
acrylic and mixed media on canvas
1983

They were playing *Manteca* and a roar crescendoed throughout the theatre...the place was wild. Through *Manteca*, Gillespie had brought the spirit of Chano Pozo to the Havana theatre and kept it there for twenty minutes. Joining Diz in this tribute to Chano was Getz, who walked out of a wing with sax in hand. Then Amram with French horn, Mantilla, Sandoval, D'Rivera, the Valdés brothers and Earl Hines played *Manteca* in bop, rock, jazz and Afro-Cuban rhythms. While his notes screeched into outer space, Sandoval compelled Diz to wave a white towel, a gesture of surrender which implied "o.k. you're the man now...the world's number one high-note specialist." It was a mind blowing experience. The Cubans were on their feet bellowing approval. It ended at 12:30 a.m. Over the din, Diz acknowledged the participating musicians. After each name there was loud applause. Then Gillespie said "Mao Tse Tung." (The noise was deafening), and the American musicians broke up with laughter.

from **RAY MANTILLA, 36 HOURS IN HAVANA**

Max Salazar

MILES DAVIS

Roland Jean

mixed media on board

1985

AFRO BLUE

Charles Searles
acrylic on canvas
1983

Miles blows blue holes thru red skies
Blistering black sounds singe the purple air
And the night is a towering orange aura hovering
above his cavernous horn

                    Miles blows down empty empires
                    while floating upon the memory
                    of a Song

Miles is a deepsea dancer
leaving acoustic trails
in green earth rhythms

                    His dramatic tone causes light
                    to appear & disappear

His trumpet is a carnivorous loa
that is fed everytime he speaks

                    His Notes crush that which cannot stand
                    its moaning weight

Miles is the eternal ruler
of the Chromatic
Spectrums of color fall from his swollen upper lip

                    Soaring symphonic syllogisms
                    race thru his fingers/are thrust
                    into the royal & open heart

A sweet scatology of beauty

FOR MILES DAVIS

Kofi Natambu

Long before I'd heard rock 'n' roll, Sarah was part of my household. I adored her. I idolized her. I found her sound—her perfect enunciation, her lavish phrasing—soothing and sensuous. Man, when Sarah sang, I swooned. I emulated her lush licks, her tasty turns, her jazz jumps, her incredible range. I loved the way she cried with her voice; I was awe-struck by her subtlety and sensitivity. No wonder they called her the Divine One. But I wondered: *Should a cat like me be singing like a chick?*

JAZZ SINGER

David Driskell
oil and collage
1974

from SMOKEY: INSIDE MY LIFE

Smokey Robinson

SARAH "SASSY" VAUGHAN AND QUINCY JONES

Jean-Pierre Leloir
photograph
1958

DINNER TIME TUNES

Mark Barry
oil on canvas
1996

it hasnt always been this way
ellington was not a street
robeson no mere memory
du bois walked up my father's stairs
hummed some tune over me
sleeping in the company of men
who changed the world

it wasnt always like this
why ray barretto used to be a side-man
& dizzy's hair was not always grey
i remember   i was there
i listened in the company of men
politics as necessary as collards
music even in our dreams

our house was filled with all kinda folks
our windows were not cement or steel
our doors opened like our daddy's arms
held us safe & loved
children growing in the company of men
old southern men & young slick ones
sonny til was not a boy
the clovers no rag-tag orphans
our crooners/ we belonged to a whole world
nkrumah was no foreigner
virgil aikens was not the only fighter

it hasnt always been this way
ellington was not a street

MOOD INDIGO

Ntozake Shange

AS KIDS GO

Sam Gilliam
acrylic on canvas, enamel on aluminum
1984-85

Drifting slowly by The Plantation, we heard an alto rise into melancholy flight on the opening bars of "Round Midnight." Confused, I thought I was hearing a record, but even that would have been a marvel: my gods—"The Bird," John Coltrane, Sonny Stitt, Sonny Rollins, Stan Getz, Cannonball Adderly—were so obscure in my town that to ask for an album by one at the music store was like asking for the latest from The Outer Mongolian Preschool Rhythm Band and Chorus in Concert.

We had stumbled onto jazz via "Moonglow with Martin" on WWL in New Orleans, and we had spent countless nights since riding in our parents' cars listening to music such as we had never dreamed existed broadcast from some twelve hundred miles away by crow-fly and a century or so by cultural disposition to our remote corner of New Mexico. Barely a decade out of its boom, our overgrown crossroad had a ragged, honky-tonk energy, but it was cowboy country, and we had begun to feel misplaced in it, practitioners of an alien religion.

MAX GORDON

Unknown
photograph
1986

from **THE PLANTATION CLUB**
C. W. Smith

SWING FAN

Charles Peterson
photograph
1938

ORNETTE HORNET

Adger W. Cowans
silver gelatin print
1986

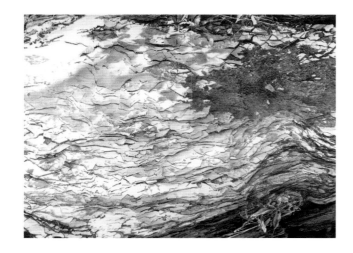

RIVERBANK: ELEGY FOR BOOKER LITTLE

Sandra De Sando

graphite on arches

1996

UNTITLED

Robert Flynt

unique-image chromogenic photograph

1991

Photographs of you at the piano are something else—like this one, taken at Birdland on one of those nights when you could play anyone else off the stand—Bird, Dizzy, anybody. Taking chorus after chorus, shoulders shrugging along with the beat, eyes closed, a vein throbbing in your temple, sweat raining on the keyboard, lips stretched back over your teeth, right hand babbling and dancing like water over rock, a foot thumping out a rhythm that got stronger and stronger as the movements of the right hand got more and more intricate, melodies blooming and fading like flowers, the momentum never easing up and then gracing effortlessly into a ballad, the keys reaching up to you, competing with each other for your touch as if the piano had been waiting a hundred years for this chance to know what it felt like to be a sax or trumpet in a black man's hands. Snarling at the audience between numbers. Hearing your name whispered wherever you went: Bud Powell, Bud Powell.

from BUT BEAUTIFUL: A BOOK ABOUT JAZZ

Geoff Dyer

I had never before thought of how awful the relationship must be between the musician and his instrument. He has to fill it, this instrument, with the breath of life, his own. He has to make it do what he wants it to do. And a piano is just a piano. It's made out of so much wood and wires and little hammers and big ones, and ivory. While there's only so much you can do with it, the only way to find this out is to try to try and make it do everything.

And Sonny hadn't been near a piano for over a year. And he wasn't on much better terms with his life, not the life that stretched before him now. He and the piano stammered, started one way, got scared, stopped; started another way, panicked, marked time, started again; then seemed to have found a direction, panicked again, got stuck. And the face I saw on Sonny I'd never seen before. Everything had been burned out of it, and, at the same time, things usually hidden were being burned in, by the fire and fury of the battle which was occurring in him up there.

Yet, watching Creole's face as they neared the end of the first set, I had the feeling that something had happened, something I hadn't heard. Then they finished, there was scattered applause, and then, without an instant's warning, Creole started into something else, it was almost sardonic, it was "Am I Blue." And, as though he commanded, Sonny began to play. Something began to happen. And Creole let out the reins. The dry, low, black man said something awful on the drums, Creole answered, and the drums talked back. Then the horn insisted, sweet and high, slightly detached perhaps, and Creole listened, commenting now and then, dry, and driving, beautiful and calm and old. Then they all came together again, and Sonny was part of the family again. I could tell this from his face. He seemed to have found, right there beneath his fingers, a damn brand-new piano. It seemed that he couldn't get over it. Then, for a while, just being happy with Sonny, they seemed to be agreeing with him that brand-new pianos certainly were a gas.

Then Creole stepped forward to remind them that what they were playing was the blues. He hit something in all of them, he hit something in me, myself, and the music tightened and deepened, apprehension began to beat the air. Creole began to tell us what the blues were all about. They were not about anything very new. He and his boys up there were keeping it new, at the risk of ruin, destruction, madness, and death, in order to find new ways to make us listen. For, while the tale of how we suffer, and how we are delighted, and how we may triumph is never new, it always must be heard. There isn't any other tale to tell, it's the only light we've got in all this darkness.

from SONNY'S BLUES

James Baldwin

5 A.M.

Gjon Mili
photograph
n.d.

JOHNNY HODGES, PARIS

Herman Leonard
photograph
1958

And that instrument could unfold softly like a flower or explode like a bomb. Traveling with it was a journey of sweet madness—standing there offstage in the magic wings each night, showered with its overpowering stomping sound, the curtain going up to ringing applause, and elegant Edward bouncing onstage smiling waving shouting we love you we love you madly then sliding under the keyboard thumping out his staccato beat as the band rose rocking and ablowing and ascreaming all around everything and everybody with Sammy Woodyard drumming hard sweating driving the wailing brass into frenzied madness and Johnny Hodges stepping out front alto sax dead center legs akimbo zombie cool eyes unfocused to infuriate the whole band with that arrogant kiss-my-ass tone of his as the brass screamed back as Edward impishly whipped up more tension Edward having fun Edward pounding Hodges higher and higher to his sharpest bossiest sound a withering onslaught blowing the phalanx of angry trumpets and trombones to gentle wailing until Cootie Williams' lone horn growled a final growl and died as Hodges contemptuously booted out his final arrogant note to applause applause and more applause with Edward smiling rising shouting Johnny Hodges Johnny Hodges Johnny Hodges. Thank you ladies and gentlemen.

from JAZZ
Gordon Parks

in memory of Papa Jo Jones
& Philly Joe Jones

There'll be all the requisites
& O how exquisite
the presence of night blooming
jazzmen & women, flowering
in aurora borealis like all the rounded
midnights & Moscow nights & New Delhi
dawns you ever wanted to drop in on
or sit in with or pencil
into your calendar of unscheduled delights.

THE BLUES ALLEY

Julia Jones
photograph
1986

There'll be love in all its liquid
power, rhythmic & brassy; mellifluous
forms, flashing flesh & the slippery
glittering skin of your teeth;
enchantment, male & female;
the orchid chords of hothouse scat
as pop song, as darkness sweetened
with light; the ascension of steps
that lead to some sumptuous Park
Avenue apartment where a bemoanable lady
lives, sophisticated to a fault, in need
of this bittersweet cultural chocolate,
this quiescent sensation of an invitation.

It'll be big, this gig called life;
the biggest. Johann Sebastian Bach
knew what it was like to bop
through a shower late in the afternoon,
then hang out in your hotel/motel/do-tell
room, wondering what time it really is
back in Iowa City or New Orleans or
the New York of all New Yorks or Rome,
the home you just left the way
autumn leaves—suddenly. Or now it's Paris
where it's going to be wine & cold sandwiches
while you're longing to dine on collard greens
& blackeyed peas with ribs & sauce
hot enough to burn away the sauerkraut &
pig's knuckle of international loneliness.

You'll make your calls & sail off
into an aria or a deep tocatta; in short
you'll honor the invitation your heart
has cabled you direct from the ace,
fulfilling all those requisite licks
so exquisite to the crowd whose deafening roar
will silence all the circus lines
the blue-hearted you never got to deliver.

It'll be the liver of life within who'll know
how *répondez s'il vous plaît* should play.
Just plan to sit & make yourself at home.

INVITATION

Al Young

UPTOWN DANCE

Ana Golobart

gouache

1992

SKY IS EVERYWHERE

Virginia Cuppaidge
acrylic and oil on canvas
1992

ACKNOWLEDGMENTS

Seeing Jazz: Artists and Writers on Jazz evolved from a series of conversations among Smithsonian staff members, jazz scholars, musicians, artists, writers, and collectors. At the core of this dialogue was the idea of a jazz aesthetic that transcends the boundaries of artistic disciplines. Whether musicians or poets, sculptors or essayists, photographers or playwrights, all artists who create in the language of jazz share certain influences, themes, and manners of expression; their works have common threads.

This book and an exhibition were developed with the aim of weaving these threads into a fascinating multicolored tapestry—of displaying together, for the first time, works of both visual art and literature tinted with the cool blues and red hot hues of jazz music.

The three co-curators who initiated this "conversation in the key of jazz" were Marquette Folley-Cooper, Deborah Macanic, and Janice McNeil. They undertook the years of research necessary to compile the "collage" of visual art and literature that served as the foundation for both this volume and the SITES traveling exhibition *Seeing Jazz.*

Many individuals have been generous in their support of this project and have added fuel to the creative processes behind the book and the exhibition. These include Robert O'Meally, who consulted on both the book and the exhibition and who also wrote the Introduction and chapter headings for the book; Michael Harris, who served as a consultant for the exhibition; Albert Murray and Myron Swartzmann, who opened aesthetic pathways during early creative dialogue; Reuben Jackson, E. Ethelbert Miller, Lisa Stewart, and Bruce Talbot, who offered their support, advice, and honest critiques; and Dorothe Rohan Dow of the Romare Bearden Foundation, Frederick Spratt, David Berger, E. Kassim Bynoe of Triangle Fine Arts International, Steve Rosenberg and Fran Kaufman of Rosenberg + Kaufman Fine Art, Norman Parish, The Sande Webster Gallery, Steve Palumbo of the Po Gallery, Mr. and Mrs. George Wein, Hermenegildo Sábat, and Marc Miller, all of whom offered their assistance during the research and compilation process.

Producing an anthology of this complexity required the efforts of a dedicated publications staff. SITES Associate Director for External Relations, Andrea Stevens, supervised the publication process. Elizabeth Goldson served as the book's editor. Andrea Hibbard provided valuable editorial support; Mark Speltz, Keira Roberts, Patsy-Ann Rasmussen, and Gillian Flory assisted in the extensive task of clearing rights and permissions. SITES would like to acknowledge Chronicle Books' continued dedication to this project, particularly the support of Senior Editor Jay Schaefer and Editorial Assistant Kate Chynoweth.

The successful realization of *Seeing Jazz* as a Smithsonian traveling exhibition was achieved by SITES Assistant Director for Programs Laurie Trippett, Project Director Sarah Tanguy, and Registrar Jane Markowitz. Early contributions to this project were made by Cynthia Haley and Anna Goiser.

Seeing Jazz is part of AMERICA'S JAZZ HERITAGE (AJH), a Partnership of the Lila Wallace-Reader's Digest Fund and the Smithsonian Institution. AJH supports a range of exhibitions, publications, and public events that promote jazz music as an original American art form. SITES Assistant Director for Programs and Co-Director of AJH, Betty Teller, championed the *Seeing Jazz* project from the beginning and worked to ensure its place in the AMERICA'S JAZZ HERITAGE program.

SITES gratefully acknowledges the writers, artists, museums, publishers, galleries, agencies, foundations, and individuals who facilitated the inclusion of one or more of the works of art and literature that appear in *Seeing Jazz.* Without their participation, neither the book nor the exhibition selected from it would have been possible.

Finally, SITES would like to thank the legendary jazz musicians Clark Terry and Milt Hinton for their support of *Seeing Jazz* and for graciously penning the foreword and afterword to this publication. We appreciate not only their important contributions to the creation of jazz but also their willingness to join the Smithsonian's effort to increase worldwide awareness and celebration of America's music.

SMITHSONIAN INSTITUTION TRAVELING EXHIBITION SERVICE (SITES)

Anna R. Cohn
Director

LIST OF ILLUSTRATIONS

We are grateful to the artists, collectors, museums, galleries, and agents who granted us permission to reprint the following works:
(Note: Dimensions are given in inches and centimeters, height by width by depth.)

Anthony Barboza
Untitled (Office Wall, Village Vanguard), 1988
Photograph
Courtesy of the artist

Anthony Barboza
Untitled (Musicians on Deck), 1983
Photograph
Courtesy of the artist

Mark Barry
Dinner Time Tunes, 1996
Oil on canvas
50 x 60 (127 x 152.4)
Collection of Mary and Steve Rose, Portland, OR

Jean-Michel Basquiat
With Strings Part 2, 1983
Acrylic and mixed media on canvas
96 x 60 (243.8 x 152.4)
Collection of The Eli Broad Family Foundation,
Santa Monica, CA

Jean-Michel Basquiat
Horn Players, 1983
Acrylic and mixed media on canvas
96 x 75 (243.8 x 190.5)
© 1983 The Estate of Jean-Michel Basquiat
Collection of Eli and Edythe L. Broad, Los Angeles, CA

Romare Bearden
Black Manhattan, 1969
Collage and synthetic polymer on board
25 3/8 x 21 (64.4 x 53.3)
Courtesy of the Art and Artifacts Division, Schomburg
Center for Research in Black Culture, The New York
Public Library, Astor, Lenox and Tilden Foundations
Photograph by Manu Sassoonian

Romare Bearden
New Orleans Farewell, 1974
Collage
44 x 60 (111.7 x 152.4)
George and Joyce Wein Collection

Romare Bearden
Jazz Village, 1967
Mixed media and collage on board
30 x 40 (76.2 x 101.6)
© Estate of Romare Bearden/Romare Bearden
Foundation, Inc.

Romare Bearden
In E Sharp, 1981
Oil and collage on paper
39 3/4 x 30 1/2 (100.9 x 77.4)
© Estate of Romare Bearden/Romare Bearden
Foundation, Inc.

Ricardo Betancourt
Eddie Palmieri, 1993
from *A Ten-Year Photo Retrospective in Latin Music*
photographs
© Ricardo Betancourt

Moe Brooker
In the Measure of Every Part, 1990
Oil on canvas
72 x 54 (182.8 x 137.1)
The Sande Webster Gallery

Moe Brooker
Gift of the Spirit, 1987
Silk screen
60 x 45 (152.4 x 114.3)
The Sande Webster Gallery

Michelle Cartaya
The Original Mambo Kings, 1993
Mixed media
12 x 16 (30.4 x 40.6)
Courtesy of the artist and Verve Records

William Claxton
Will Shade and his Tub Bass, Memphis, 1960
Silver gelatin print
© William Claxton

William Claxton
Chet Baker and Teddy Charles, Pasadena, 1953
Silver gelatin print
© William Claxton

Miguel Covarrubias
The Lindy Hop, 1936
Lithograph
The Metropolitan Museum of Art
Harris Brisbane Dick Fund, 1940

Adger W. Cowans
Ornette Hornet, 1986
Silver gelatin print
Courtesy of the artist

Michael Cummings
African Jazz Series, 1990
Four quilts, each 108 x 72 (274.3 x 182.8)
Courtesy of the artist

Virginia Cuppaidge
Sky is Everywhere, 1992
Acrylic and oil on canvas
73 1/2 x 97 1/2 (186.6 x 247.6)
Courtesy Rosenberg + Kaufman Fine Art, NYC
Photograph by D. James Dee

Stuart Davis
Pad No. 4, 1947
Silk-screen reproduction
14 x 18 (35.5 x 45.7)
Courtesy Earl Davis

Alexis De Boeck
Untitled, No. 29, 1987
Oil pastel on paper
40 x 32 (101.6 x 81.2)
© Evelyn De Boeck
Courtesy of William and Joyce O'Brien

Charles Demuth
Negro Jazz Band, 1916
Watercolor on paper
13 x 8 (33 x 20.3)
Courtesy Dr. Irwin Goldstein

Sandra De Sando
Riverbank: Elegy for Booker Little, 1996
Graphite on arches
22 x 30 (55.8 x 76.2)
Courtesy of the artist
Photograph by Jellybean Photographics

David Driskell
Jazz Singer, 1974
Oil and collage
56 x 48 (142.2 x 121.9)
Collection of the artist
Photograph by Gregory R. Staley

Jean Dubuffet
Grand Jazz Band (New Orleans) from the *Marionettes de la ville et de la campagne* series, 1944
Oil and tempera on canvas
45 1/8 x 57 3/4 (114.6 x 146.6)
The Museum of Modern Art, New York
Gift of Nina and Gordon Bunshaft
Photograph © 1997 The Museum of Modern Art, New York

David Ellis
Preservation Hall, 1993
India ink on paper
10 x 14 (25.4 x 35.5)
Collection of Natalie Cash

Robert Flynt
Untitled, 1991
Unique-image chromogenic photograph
Courtesy of the artist and the Witkin Gallery, New York

Lee Friedlander
Sweet Emma Barrett, 1958
Silver gelatin print
Courtesy Fraenkel Gallery, San Francisco

Jean Perschbacher Fujio
I'd Rather Be Sharp Than a B Flat, 1993
Fiber
46 x 49 (116.8 x 124.4)
Courtesy of the artist and Po Gallery, Providence, RI
Photograph by Davis Caras

Juan Alberto Garcia de Cubas
Esperando un poco (Waiting a Little), 1993
Collage with watercolor, pencil, ink, and photocopy
41 1/2 x 30 (105.4 x 76.2)
Courtesy of the artist

Sam Gilliam
As Kids Go, 1984-85
Acrylic on canvas, enamel on aluminum
55 x 67 x 4 (139.7 x 170.1 x 10.1)
Courtesy of the artist and Baumgartner Galleries,
Washington, DC
Photograph by Mark Gulezian/QuickSilver

Lynn Goldsmith
The Eye of the Horn (Wynton Marsalis), 1993
Mamiya
© Lynn Goldsmith

Ana Golobart
Uptown Dance, 1992
Gouache
9 x 12 (22.8 x 30.4)
© Ana Golobart

William P. Gottlieb
Ella Fitzgerald and Dizzy Gillespie, 1947
Photograph
© William P. Gottlieb

William P. Gottlieb
Minton's (Thelonious Monk, Howard McGhee, Roy Eldridge, Teddy Hill), 1946
Photograph
© William P. Gottlieb

William P. Gottlieb
Nick's (Pee Wee Russell, Muggsy Spanier, Miff Mole, Joe Grauso), 1946
Photograph
© William P. Gottlieb

Robert Graham
Untitled (Digitized Section of Duke Ellington), 1988
Wax
17 3/4 h. (45 h.)
Courtesy of the artist

Jarvis Grant
Dexter Gordon, 1989
Silver print
© Jarvis Grant

Palmer Hayden
Cafe L'Avenue, 1932
Watercolor and graphite on paper
9 1/2 x 7 1/2 (24.1 x 19)
Courtesy of the Corcoran Museum and the Evans-Tibbs
Collection of African American Art

Milt Hinton
Cozy Cole, Danny Barker, and Shad Collins, New Orleans, c. 1941
Photograph
© Milt Hinton

Milt Hinton
Lester Young and J. C. Heard, Harlem, 1958
Photograph
© Milt Hinton

J. Michael Howard
We Came to Play, 1992
Acrylic on canvas
16 x 14 (40.6 x 35.5)
Courtesy of the artist

Wadsworth Jarrell
Basie at the Apollo, 1992
Acrylic on canvas
59 x 72 (149.8 x 182.8)
The Sande Webster Gallery
Photograph by Wadsworth Jarrell

Roland Jean
Mona Lisa, 1985
Mixed media on board
48 x 48 (121.9 x 121.9)
Collection of Hazel Da Breo, Toronto

Roland Jean
Miles Davis, 1985
Mixed media on board
48 x 96 (121.9 x 243.8)
Courtesy of the artist

Julia Jones
The Blues Alley, 1986
Photograph
© 1986 Julia Jones

Hughie Lee-Smith
Slum Song, 1960
Oil on canvas
27 x 30 (68.5 x 76.2)
Courtesy of Golden State Mutual Life Insurance Company

Jean-Pierre Leloir
Sarah "Sassy" Vaughan and Quincy Jones, 1958
Photograph
Courtesy of the artist

Herman Leonard
Gerry Mulligan, Zoot Sims, Mercury Recording Studio, NYC, 1955
Photograph
© 1955 Herman Leonard

Herman Leonard
Duke Ellington and Benny Goodman Listen to Ella Fitzgerald, 1949
Photograph
© 1949 Herman Leonard

Herman Leonard
Johnny Hodges, Paris, 1958
Photograph
© 1958 Herman Leonard

Norman Lewis
Untitled (Sketch to Charlie Parker's Music), 1949
Pen, ink, and wash on paper
19 x 24 (48.2 x 60.9)
Courtesy E. Kassim Bynoe/Tarin M. Fuller
Photograph by Ali Elai

Norman Lewis
Street Music, Jenkins Band, 1944
Oil on canvas
27 x 45 (68.5 x 114.3)
Courtesy of the Art and Artifacts Division, Schomburg Center for Research in Black Culture, The New York Public Library, Astor, Lenox and Tilden Foundations
Photograph by Manu Sassoonian

Norman Lewis
Harlem Jazz Jamboree, 1943
Oil on canvas
18 x 16 (45.7 x 40.6)
George and Joyce Wein Collection
Photograph by Jim Strong

Peter Wayne Lewis
Black Swan Suite, 1993
Oil on canvas
Installation of 15 paintings, each 30 x 22 (76.2 x 55.8)
Courtesy Rosenberg + Kaufman Fine Art, NYC

Ed Love
The Strutters, 1986
Polychromed welded steel
Four elements, each 70 to 76 h. (177.8 to 193 h.)
Courtesy of the artist
Photograph by Charles Badland

Ed Love
Alabama, 1993
Welded steel
40 x 25 x 12 (101.6 x 63.5 x 30.4)
Courtesy of the artist
Photograph by Scott Brightwell

Henri Matisse
Icarus, Plate VIII from *Jazz* by Henri Matisse. Paris, E. Tériade, 1947
Pochoir, printed in color, each double page: 16 5/8 x 25 5/8 (42.2 x 65)
The Museum of Modern Art, New York
The Louis E. Stern Collection
Photograph © 1997 The Museum of Modern Art, New York

Gjon Mili
5 A.M., n.d.
Photograph
Courtesy Life Magazine
© Time Inc.

Tom Miller
Pretty Pretty, 1995
Acrylic on wood with phonograph record, boots, fake fur, and metal spring
54 3/4 x 26 x 18 3/4 (139 x 66 x 48)
Courtesy Robyn Thompson
Photograph by Carl Clark

Morgan Monceaux
Art Tatum, 1991
Mixed media
30 x 22 1/2 (76.2 x 57.1)
Collection of Morgan Rank
Courtesy of Morgan Rank Gallery

Morgan Monceaux
Bessie Smith, 1993
Mixed media
30 x 22 1/2 (76.2 x 57.1)
Collection of Morgan Rank
Courtesy of Morgan Rank Gallery

Piet Mondrian
Broadway Boogie Woogie, 1942-43
Oil on canvas
50 x 50 (127 x 127)
The Museum of Modern Art, New York
Given anonymously
Photograph ©1997 The Museum of Modern Art, New York

Archibald J. Motley, Jr.
Hot Rhythm, 1961
Oil on canvas
40 x 48 3/8 (101.6 x 122.8)
Collection of Archie Motley and Valerie Gerrard Browne

Archibald J. Motley, Jr.
After Fiesta, Remorse, Siesta, 1959-60
Oil on canvas
33 x 38 (83.8 x 96.5)
Courtesy Teresa Grana and Thurlow Evans Tibbs, Jr.

Nobou Nakamura
Jazz Musicians, 1983
Photograph
Courtesy of the artist

Ademola Olugebefola
Sun Ra, 1994
Mixed media
36 x 26 (91.4 x 66)
Courtesy Triangle Fine Arts International

Robert Parent
Addison and Art Farmer, 1955
Silver gelatin print
Courtesy Dale Parent, The Bob Parent Archive

Gordon Parks
Untitled (Musician's Feet with Mutes), 1960
Photograph
Courtesy of the artist

Charles Peterson
Swing Fan, 1938
Photograph
Courtesy Don Peterson

James Phillips
Drum Thing (No Blues for Elvin), 1995
Acrylic on paper
60 x 22 (152.4 x 55.8)
Courtesy of the artist
Photograph by Raymond Lee Photography

Tom Phillips
Jazz on a Summer's Day, 1977
Charcoal and pastel on paper
47 1/4 x 29 1/2 (120 x 74.9)
Courtesy of the artist
Photograph by Bill Hurrell

Letizia Pitigliani
Morning Note, 1989
Acrylic on canvas
100 x 96 (254 x 243.8)
© Letizia Pitigliani

Archie Rand
Gene Ammons / Archie Shepp, 1970
Acrylic resin and mixed media on canvas
17 x 68 1/4 (43.1 x 173.3)
Collection of the artist
Photograph by Peter Muscato

Man Ray
Jazz, c. 1919
Tempera and ink (aerograph) on paper
28 x 22 (71.1 x 55.8)
Columbus Museum of Art, Ohio
Gift of Ferdinand Howald

Noel Rockmore
Memory of Punch Miller, 1963
Oil on masonite
20 x 15 (50.8 x 38.1)
George and Joyce Wein Collection
Photograph by Jim Strong

Mahler Ryder
Toshiko, 1990
Wood and acrylic paint
52 x 61 x 2 (132 x 154.9 x 5)
Courtesy Po Gallery, Providence, RI
Photograph by Roger Birn

Hermenegildo Sábat
Band Member at Bebé Ridgley's Funeral, 1961
Photograph
Courtesy of the artist

Raymond Saunders
Blues, Red, Yellow II (Homage to Billie Holiday), 1990
Oil, mixed media on wood
Two panels with total size of 48 x 79 1/2 (121.9 x 201.9)
Courtesy of the artist and Stephen Wirtz Gallery, San Francisco
Photograph by Ben Blackwell

Raymond Saunders
The Gift of Presence, 1993-94
Mixed media on wood
Six panels, each 10 1/4 x 8 1/4 (26 x 20.9)
Collection of the Oakland Museum
Gift of The Collectors Gallery

Randall Schmit
Magus Mantis, 1989
Oil, acrylic, pastel, and graphite on canvas
72 x 72 (182.8 x 182.8)
Courtesy of the artist
Collection of Timothy A. Foley, New Orleans

John T. Scott
Stage Door No Exit, 1995
Polychromed aluminum
27 x 24 x 13 1/2 (68.5 x 60.9 x 34.2)
Courtesy of Galerie Simonne Stern, New Orleans
Photograph by Judy Cooper

Charles Searles
Freedom's Gate, 1992
Bronze
12 x 8 x 3 (30.4 x 20.3 x 7.6)
Courtesy of the artist
Photograph by Jack Ramsdale

Charles Searles
Striving, 1994
Bronze
14 x 8 x 3 (35.5 x 20.3 x 7.6)
Courtesy of the artist
Photograph by Jack Ramsdale

Charles Searles
Warrior, 1992
Bronze
18 x 8 x 4 (45.7 x 20.3 x 10.1)
Courtesy of the artist
Photograph by Jack Ramsdale

Charles Searles
Afro Blue, 1983
Acrylic on canvas
54 x 44 (137.1 x 111.7)
Collection of the artist

Al Smith
Bembé Clavé, 1994
Mixed media
59 x 52 (149.8 x 132)
Courtesy of the artist
Photograph by John Pinderhughes

Eugene Smith
As from My Window I Sometimes Glance, 1957-58
Silver gelatin print
Courtesy Eugene Smith/Black Star

Frank Smith
The Cabinet of Dr. Buzzard, 1983
Acrylic painting with collage on paper
60 x 52 (152.4 x 132)
Courtesy Parish Gallery, Washington, DC

Vincent Smith
On the Road, 1989
Monotype
38 x 50 (96.5 x 127)
Courtesy G.W. Einstein Gallery, New York

Dennis Stock
Billie Holiday, 1958
Photograph
Courtesy Dennis Stock/Magnum Photos

Dennis Stock
Mary Lou Williams at her Piano, 1958
Photograph
Courtesy Dennis Stock/Magnum Photos

Dennis Stock
Anita O'Day, 1958
Photograph
Courtesy Dennis Stock/Magnum Photos

Dennis Stock
Still Life (Louis Armstrong's Horn Case), 1958
Photograph
Courtesy Dennis Stock/Magnum Photos

Mark Taber
Black and Tan, 1994
Mixed media
75 x 44 x 24 (190.5 x 111.7 x 60.9)
Courtesy Po Gallery, Providence, RI
Photograph by Roger Birn

Ann Tanksley
Dancing Couple No. 2, 1992
Oil on canvas
14 x 11 (35.5 x 27.9)
Collection of the artist

Laura Thorne
Great Expectations, 1995
Mixed media
27 x 6 x 6 (68.5 x 15.2 x 15.2)
Courtesy Rosenberg + Kaufman Fine Art, NYC
Photograph by Brad Miller

William Tolliver
Transcendent of the Blues, 1992
Oil on canvas
108 x 72 (274.3 x 182.8)
Collection of the artist

Unknown
Max Gordon, 1986
Photograph
Collection of Lorraine Gordon

Douglas Vogel
Yellow Dog Blues, 1995
Mixed media with electric light
80 3/4 x 97 1/4 x 4 (205.1 x 247 x 10.1)
Courtesy Frederick Spratt Gallery, San Jose, CA, and the artist

Douglas Vogel
Blue Light (for Duke Ellington), 1981-82
Mixed media with electric light
67 1/2 x 36 5/8 x 4 1/2 (171.4 x 93 x 11.4)
Courtesy Frederick Spratt Gallery, San Jose, CA, and the artist

Denise Ward-Brown
Sing Praises, 1993
Assemblage
40 x 20 x 17 (101.6 x 50.8 x 43.1)
Collection of the artist
Photograph by Red Elf

Billy Dee Williams
Oop-pop-a-da, 1994
Mixed media on paper
18 x 12 (45.7 x 30.4)
Courtesy of the artist

William T. Williams
Carolina Shout, 1990
Acrylic on canvas
75 x 44 (190.5 x 111.7)
Courtesy of the artist
George and Joyce Wein Collection
Photograph by Josh Neasky

LITERARY PERMISSIONS

PRETTY PRETTY

Tom Miller
mixed media
1995

INDEX OF ARTISTS AND WRITERS

AFTERWORD

Over the years I've been asked why I took some of the photos I did. I think my answer surprises many people. When I took those early pictures of Dizzy Gillespie, we were both in Cab Calloway's band. Even back in those days I knew he was an innovator, but I never suspected that he would become a jazz legend. The same is true for other guys who were in the band like Ben Webster, Chu Berry, and Cozy Cole. They were my friends, and I wanted pictures of them so that, one day, we could all look back and remember the good times we shared in our youth.

At some point, probably in the early 1950s, I began to realize that I was experiencing jazz history firsthand. The music was changing rapidly, and new faces were always coming on the scene. Some of the greats, like Chu and Jimmy Blanton, were already gone, and others were well on their way to early deaths. I felt strongly about using my camera to capture some of the people and events that I was lucky enough to witness.

When I first started taking photographs I really didn't think about creating art. I was just a musician who happened to have a camera and wanted to document aspects of the jazz world I knew—on the road, backstage, at recording and T.V. studios, and festivals.

I began to see my photographs as art because, in recent years, they have been shown in museums and galleries and many people see them that way.

I've come to believe that art—in all of its forms—can reveal and preserve the spirit and essence of jazz, so that present and future generations can experience it.

Milt Hinton